T0220603

Raspbian OS Programming with the Raspberry Pi

IoT Projects with Wolfram, Mathematica, and Scratch

Agus Kurniawan

Apress®

Raspbian OS Programming with the Raspberry Pi: IoT Projects with Wolfram, Mathematica, and Scratch

Agus Kurniawan
Depok, Indonesia

ISBN-13 (pbk): 978-1-4842-4211-7   ISBN-13 (electronic): 978-1-4842-4212-4
https://doi.org/10.1007/978-1-4842-4212-4

Library of Congress Control Number: 2018964829

Managing Director, Apress Media LLC: Welmoed Spahr
Acquisitions Editor: Natalie Pao
Development Editor: James Markham
Coordinating Editor: Jessica Vakili

Cover image designed by Freepik (www.freepik.com)

Distributed to the book trade worldwide by Springer Science+Business Media New York, 233 Spring Street, 6th Floor, New York, NY 10013. Phone 1-800-SPRINGER, fax (201) 348-4505, e-mail orders-ny@springer-sbm.com, or visit www.springeronline.com. Apress Media, LLC is a California LLC and the sole member (owner) is Springer Science + Business Media Finance Inc (SSBM Finance Inc). SSBM Finance Inc is a **Delaware** corporation.

For information on translations, please e-mail rights@apress.com, or visit http://www.apress.com/rights-permissions.

Apress titles may be purchased in bulk for academic, corporate, or promotional use. eBook versions and licenses are also available for most titles. For more information, reference our Print and eBook Bulk Sales web page at http://www.apress.com/bulk-sales.

Any source code or other supplementary material referenced by the author in this book is available to readers on GitHub via the book's product page, located at www.apress.com/978-1-4842-4211-7. For more detailed information, please visit http://www.apress.com/source-code.

Printed on acid-free paper

Table of Contents

About the Author

Agus Kurniawan is a lecturer, researcher, IT consultant, and an author. He has 17 years of experience in various software and hardware development projects, delivering materials in training and workshops, and technical writing. He has been awarded the Microsoft Most Valuable Professional (MVP) award 14 years in a row.

His topic interests are software engineering, embedded system, networking, and security system. He has been working as lecturer and researcher at the Faculty of Computer Science, Universitas Indonesia. Currently, he is pursuing a PhD in computer science at the Freie Universität Berlin, Germany. He can be reached on his blog at http://blog.aguskurniawan.net and Twitter at @agusk2010.

About the Technical Reviewer

Massimo Nardone has more than 22 years of experiences in security, web/mobile development, cloud, and IT architecture. His true IT passions are security and Android.

He has been programming and teaching how to program with Android, Perl, PHP, Java, VB, Python, C/C++, and MySQL for more than 20 years.

He holds a Master of Science degree in Computing Science from the University of Salerno, Italy.

He has worked as a Project Manager, Software Engineer, Research Engineer, Chief Security Architect, Information Security Manager, PCI/SCADA Auditor, and Senior Lead IT Security/Cloud/SCADA Architect for many years.

Technical skills include: Security, Android, Cloud, Java, MySQL, Drupal, Cobol, Perl, web and mobile development, MongoDB, D3, Joomla, Couchbase, C/C++, WebGL, Python, Pro Rails, Django CMS, Jekyll, Scratch, etc.

He currently works as Chief Information Security Office (CISO) for Cargotec Oyj.

Acknowledgments

We would like to thank Apress for all their help in making this book possible. Specifically, we would like to thank Aaron Black, our acquisitions editor, and Jessica Vakili, our coordinating editor, for helping us complete the Raspbian book.

Special thanks to our development editor, James Markham, and technical reviewers, Chaim Krause and Massimo Nardone, for all of their suggestions during the editorial review process that helped make this a great book.

We would also like to thank the Raspberry Pi and Raspbian communities anywhere in the world for contributing and making learning Raspberry Pi with Raspbian easy.

Last but not least, a thank you to my wife, Ela and my children, Thariq and Zahra, for their great support while I completed this book.

Introduction

Raspberry Pi is a mini computer that you can operate as a normal computer. The Raspberry Pi board is one of recommended development boards with IoT platforms. There are many features on the Raspbian OS and Raspberry Pi boards that you can use to build IoT programs in various scenarios. Raspberry Pi is designed to enable you to scale its capabilities through GPIO pins that are suitable for your business and research needs.

Raspbian OS Programming with the Raspberry Pi is a quick reference to build programs on top of the Raspbian OS on a Raspberry Pi board. You'll start by learning Raspbian shells to develop programs. You will go through a step-by-step guide with project samples to learn the ins and outs of the Raspbian OS development. You will also learn about the Wolfram language, Mathematica, and Scratch.

Who This Book Is For

This book is designed for anyone who wants to get started with Raspberry Pi and Raspbian. Readers do not need knowledge of the Linux OS or of embedded systems.

How This Book Is Organized

This book is designed with a step-by-step approach. You will learn how to set up Raspbian on a Raspberry Pi board. You will also learn how to develop programs on Raspbian. This book explains how to work with Wolfram, Mathematica, and Scratch. Some scenario problems are provided so you can practice during the learning process.

Required Software, Materials, and Equipment

In general, you need a Raspberry Pi 3 board and a microSD card with Raspbian OS installed. All required software in this book is installed with the Raspbian OS.

CHAPTER 1

Introduction to Raspberry Pi

Raspberry Pi is a development board that can be applied to build IoT applications. Various sensors and actuator devices can be attached to the board. In this chapter, we explore Raspberry Pi and cover its models. We also learn how to set up the board for the first time.

The following list of topics is covered in this chapter:

- Learn about the Raspberry Pi

- Review the Raspberry Pi models

- Learn about the Raspbian OS

- Set up Raspbian OS on a Raspberry Pi board

- Perform headless Raspbian SSH network setup

- Configure a WiFi network

- Explore the Raspbian OS desktop

- Configure the VNC server

- Learn to power off the Raspbian

© Agus Kurniawan 2019
A. Kurniawan, *Raspbian OS Programming with the Raspberry Pi*,
https://doi.org/10.1007/978-1-4842-4212-4_1

1.1 What Is Raspberry Pi?

Raspberry Pi is a mini computer that you can operate as a normal computer. This board was developed by Raspberry Pi Foundation in the UK. Currently, Raspberry Pi runs on the top of an ARM processor. Raspberry Pi is not a PC, so we couldn't expect more in computation. Raspberry Pi is designed to be small in size to perform some processes. The small form size of the Raspberry Pi form has advantages. We can put sensor and actuator devices on the Raspberry Pi board and then perform measurement and sensing.

The first Raspberry Pi Model B board was released in February 2012. The latest model is the Raspberry Pi 3 B+ board and it was released in March 2018. You can see this board in Figure 1-1. This board can run an operating system to perform computations.

Figure 1-1. *Raspberry Pi 3 B+ board*

The Raspberry Pi board usually exposes GPIO pins, to which we can attach sensors or actuator devices. Some Raspberry Pi models also provide network stacks such as Ethernet, WiFi, and Bluetooth. Raspberry Pi can also be connected to monitor through an HDMI connector.

Various operating systems can be applied to Raspberry Pi boards. A list of supported operating systems for Raspberry Pi can be found at this site: `https://www.raspberrypi.org/downloads/`. Raspbian OS is the official operating system of the Raspberry Pi. This book focuses on Raspbian OS for implementation and evaluation.

1.2 Reviewing the Raspberry Pi Board Models

There are several Raspberry Pi models that we can use to perform specific purposes. The latest model as I am writing this book is Raspberry Pi 3 Model B+. This board consists of Broadcom BCM2837B0, Cortex-A53 (ARMv8) 64-bit SoC @ 1.4GHz, with 1GB LPDDR2 SDRAM. The board also provides Ethernet, WiFi, and Bluetooth 4.2 (BLE). You can see the Raspberry Pi 3 Model B+ board in Figure 1-1. For further information about Raspberry Pi 3 Model B+, see `https://www.raspberrypi.org/products/raspberry-pi-3-model-b-plus/`.

If you have concerns about hardware size, Raspberry Pi Foundation has an even smaller version, which is half the size of a credit card. It is called the Raspberry Pi Zero. There are two models—Raspberry Pi Zero and Raspberry Pi Zero Wireless. The first model was released in November 2015. The last model that has a WiFi module was released in February 2017. Both models run Broadcom BCM2835 MCU with 512MB RAM. You can see the Raspberry Pi Zero Wireless board form in Figure 1-2.

Figure 1-2. *Raspberry Pi Zero Wireless board*

You also can see and compare several Raspberry Pi models based on processor, RAM, and network module availability in Table 1-1.

Table 1-1. *Raspberry Pi Model Comparison*

Raspberry Pi Model	Processor	RAM	Network Modules
Raspberry Pi 3 B+	Broadcom BCM2837B0	1GB	Ethernet, WiFi, BLE
Raspberry Pi Zero Wireless	Broadcom BCM2835	512MB	WiFi
Raspberry Pi 3	Broadcom BCM2837	1GB	Ethernet, WiFi, BLE
Raspberry Pi Zero	Broadcom BCM2835	512MB	-
Raspberry Pi 2	Broadcom BCM2836	1GB	Ethernet
Raspberry Pi A+	Broadcom BCM2835	256MB	-
Raspberry Pi B	Broadcom BCM2835	512MB	Ethernet

Technically, all the Raspberry Pi models that are shown in Table 1-1 are designed for personal makers and hobbyists. There are limited GPIO pins on each Raspberry Pi model. If you need more GPIO pins on the board, you can extend it using GPIO extender modules. The Raspberry Pi Foundation also released the Raspberry Pi model for industry purposes. It is called the Raspberry Pi Compute Module. Currently, the latest model is Raspberry Pi Compute Module V3.

Raspberry Pi Compute Module V3 board hosts 120 GPIO pins, an HDMI port, a USB port, two camera ports, and two display ports. You can see the board form in Figure 1-3. For further information about the Raspberry Pi Compute Module V3, visit the official website at http:// socialcompare.com/en/comparison/raspberrypi-models-comparison.

Figure 1-3. *Raspberry Pi Compute Module v3*

1.3 Introducing the Raspbian OS

Raspbian is an operating system-based Debian optimized for the Raspberry Pi hardware. When the Raspberry Pi board is released, Raspbian OS becomes the official OS for Raspberry Pi boards. Raspbian OS is an open source operating system that was initiated by Mike Thompson and Peter Green. The official Raspbian project can be found on this site: https://www.raspbian.org/.

If you have experience using Debian and Ubuntu Linux, you should be familiar with Raspbian OS since this OS is built based on Debian Linux and optimized on a Raspberry Pi board with ARMv6 CPU.

This book uses Raspbian OS for testing and evaluation. You can download the Raspbian image file at `https://www.raspberrypi.org/downloads`. Currently, Raspbian provides desktop and lite versions. You can see the download image in Figure 1-4. The Raspbian desktop version is running Raspbian OS with an installed desktop runtime. The Raspbian lite version is designed for light usage. It means you will obtain the Terminal runtime.

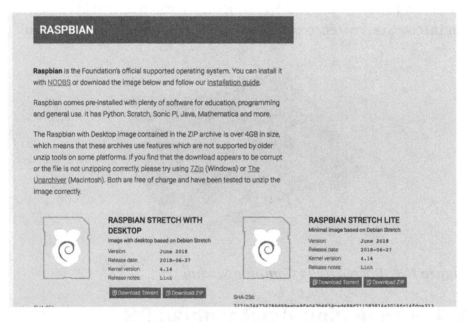

Figure 1-4. *Download the Raspbian OS image*

Next, I show you how to set up Raspbian OS on the Raspberry Pi 3 board.

1.4 Setting Up Raspbian OS on Raspberry Pi Boards

The Raspberry Pi models don't have internal storage unless you're using the Raspberry Pi Compute Module. You should attach external storage, such as an SD card or a microSD card. The new Raspberry Pi board model uses microSD for external storage.

I recommended that you use a microSD card that's 16GB. You can install some libraries, frameworks, and tools for your personal and business needs. In this section, I'm going to show you how to set up Raspbian OS on a Raspberry Pi 3 board.

First, download the Raspbian OS image. You can download it at `https://www.raspberrypi.org/downloads`. For demo purposes, I chose the Raspbian Stretch with desktop, as shown in Figure 1-4. To flash the Raspbian image into the microSD card, you can use Etcher. It's free and available for Windows, Mac, and Linux. You can see the Etcher application in Figure 1-5. Download it from `https://etcher.io`, based on your platform, and then install it.

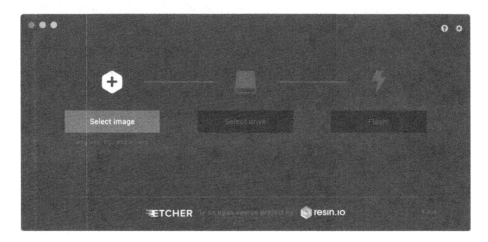

Figure 1-5. *Etcher application*

The Etcher application is easy to use. You can just select your Raspbian image and target the drive of the microSD card on your computer. Some computers don't have microSD card readers, so you need an SDcard reader. Then put your microSD card into the reader.

After completing the flashing Raspbian step, you can plug your keyboard, mouse, and monitor into the Raspberry Pi board.

Details about Raspbian installation on the Raspberry Pi board can be found in the official guideline manual at `https://www.raspberrypi.org/documentation/installation/installing-images/README.md`.

1.5 Headless Raspbian SSH Network Setup

Sometimes you won't want to use a keyboard or monitor to manage the Raspbian network. We can perform a headless Raspbian network in this case. In this scenario, the Raspberry Pi board will be connected to a network via Ethernet. You'll want to enable an SSH service on the Raspberry Pi without configuring your keyboard and monitor.

First, load your Raspbian microSD card into your computer. You should see a Raspbian drive. Now you want to enable SSH on Raspbian. You can create a file, called `ssh` without a file extension, with blank content. Put this file into the Raspbian drive. You can see it in Figure 1-6.

After you're done, you should plug the Raspbian microSD card into the Raspberry Pi board. Plug your LAN cable into the Raspberry Pi Ethernet connector. After that, turn on your Raspberry Pi board.

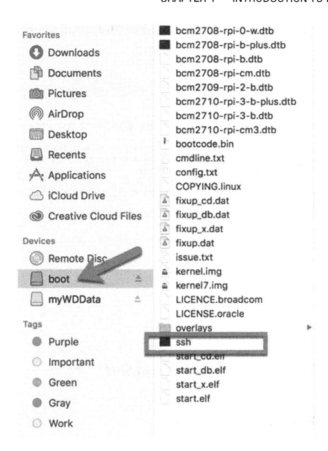

Figure 1-6. *Adding an ssh file into Raspbian disk*

Wait several minutes to ensure Raspbian has started. You should get your Raspbian IP address from your router. Now open the SSH client application. For Windows, you can use the PuTTY application at https://www.putty.org. For Linux and Mac, you can use the Terminal. For instance, the Raspbian IP address is 192.168.1.21 and the username is pi. Then type this command.

```
$ ssh pi@192.168.1.21
```

You should be able to access the Raspbian Terminal remotely. You can see an example of remote SSH in Figure 1-7.

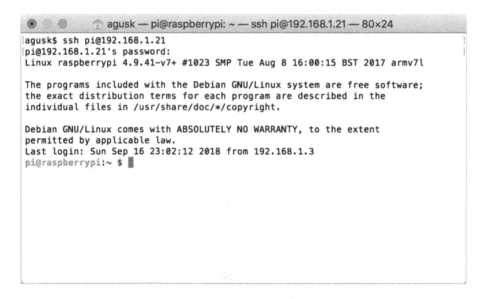

Figure 1-7. *Connecting to Raspbian via SSH*

1.6 Expanding Storage

Before you install any libraries, frameworks, or tools, I recommend that you expand the Raspbian disk. You can open Raspbian Terminal from the desktop or by using remote SSH. Type this command.

```
$ sudo raspi-config
```

You should see the form shown in Figure 1-8.

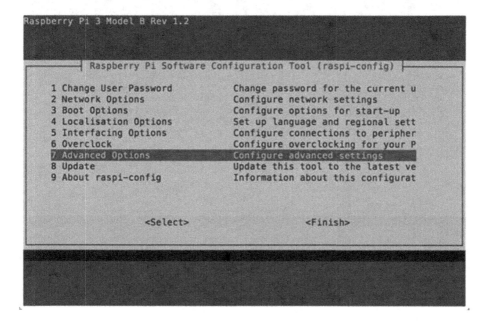

Figure 1-8. *Select Advanced Options*

From the main menu (see Figure 1-8), you can select the Advanced Options menu. Then, you should see the form that is shown in Figure 1-9.

Select the Expand Filesystem option. After that, you will obtain confirmation. If you're done, Raspbian will expand your disk.

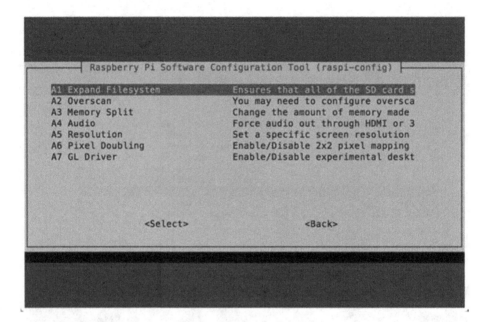

Figure 1-9. Expand the filesystem

1.7 Configuring a WiFi Network

Raspberry Pi 3 has a built-in WiFi network. You can connect this WiFI to existing WiFi networks. If you are working on the Raspbian Desktop, you can see the WiFi icon on the top right. Figure 1-10 shows an arrow pointing to the connect WiFi option.

Figure 1-10. *Connect to existing WiFi*

After you select one of the WiFi SSIDs, you probably will be asked for the SSID pin. Fill in the SSID pin and then your Raspbian will connect to the network.

1.8 Exploring the Raspbian OS Desktop and Terminal

The Raspbian OS desktop has a look and feel like other operating systems. Some applications have been installed for you, such as the Chrome browser, Wolfram, Mathematica. A form of the Raspbian OS can be seen in Figure 1-11.

Figure 1-11. *Raspbian Scratch OS desktop on Raspberry Pi 3*

If you click on the Raspberry Pi logo on the top-left, you should see a main menu, as shown in Figure 1-12. You can see a list of applications and the managing systems.

Figure 1-12. *Main menu on Raspbian desktop OS*

For instance, open a browser from the Internet menu. You can surf the Internet as you do in a normal browser. Raspbian installed Chromium as its default browser application. You can see this browser in Figure 1-13.

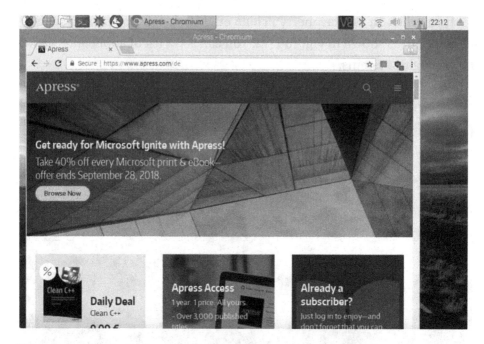

Figure 1-13. Opening a browser for Internet access

1.9 Configuring the VNC Server

You will probably access Raspbian desktop remotely, so you don't need to use the keyboard and monitor to access the Raspbian desktop. In this section, we install the VNC server. An Internet network is required to perform this task. Make sure your Raspberry Pi has connected to the Internet via a LAN or a WiFi network.

To do this, you will perform these steps:

1. Install the VNC server.

2. Enable the VNC server.

3. Configure the boot option for desktop.

4. Test with the VNC viewer.

Each task is presented in detail in the following sections.

1.9.1 Installing the VNC Server

To install the VNC server on Raspberry Pi 3, you can perform this task on the Terminal. First, open the Terminal via SSH. After that, type these commands.

```
$ sudo apt-get update
$ sudo apt-get install realvnc-vnc-server realvnc-vnc-viewer
```

This task will download and install the VNC server and viewer application on to your Raspbian.

1.9.2 Enabling the VNC Server

The next step is to enable the VNC server on the Raspbian. You can do this step via the Terminal. You can type this command.

```
$ sudo raspi-config
```

After the command is executed, you should see the form shown previously in Figure 1-8. Select Interfacing Options. You should then see the menu shown in Figure 1-14. From there, select VNC.

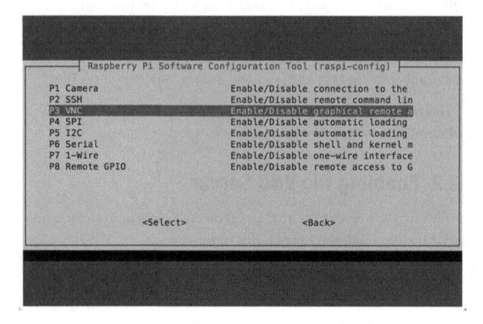

Figure 1-14. *Selecting VNC*

Next, you are asked to confirm that you want to enable the VNC server, as shown in Figure 1-15. Select Yes.

Figure 1-15. *Confirmation for enabling the VNC server*

Next, you need to enable the boot options for the desktop.

1.9.3 Configuring Boot Options for the Desktop

Since VNC remote needs desktop service, we should configure Raspbian to enable it running in desktop mode. You can configure this via `raspi-config`. You can call it via the Terminal.

```
$ sudo raspi-config
```

After it's executed, you should get the form shown in Figure 1-16. Select Boot Options so you will have a form, as shown in Figure 1-17.

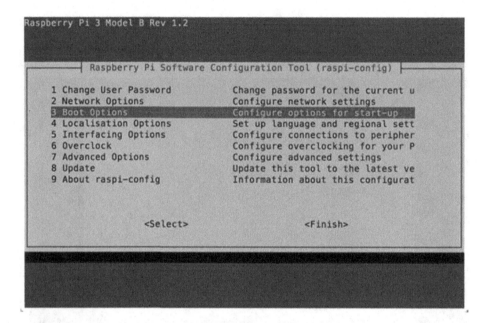

Figure 1-16. *Selecting Boot Options*

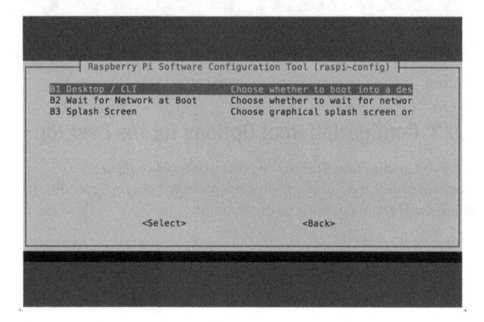

Figure 1-17. *Selecting Desktop/CLI*

Now you can select Desktop Autologin, as shown in Figure 1-18.

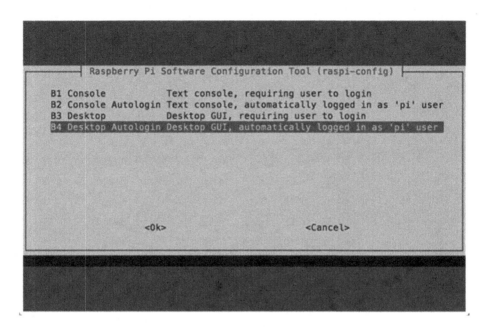

Figure 1-18. *Selecting Desktop Autologin Desktop GUI*

When you're done, your Raspbian will reboot.

1.9.4 Testing the Server

To test the VNC server, you need to install a VNC client. We can use the VNC Viewer application to do this. You can download this application based on your platform from https://www.realvnc.com/en/connect/download/viewer/.

You can see VNC Viewer application in Figure 1-19. This application is easier to use.

Figure 1-19. *VNC Viewer application on the Mac platform*

Now you can type the IP address of Raspbian into the textbox of the VNC Viewer application. If you're connected, you will be asked to provide the username and password, as shown in Figure 1-20.

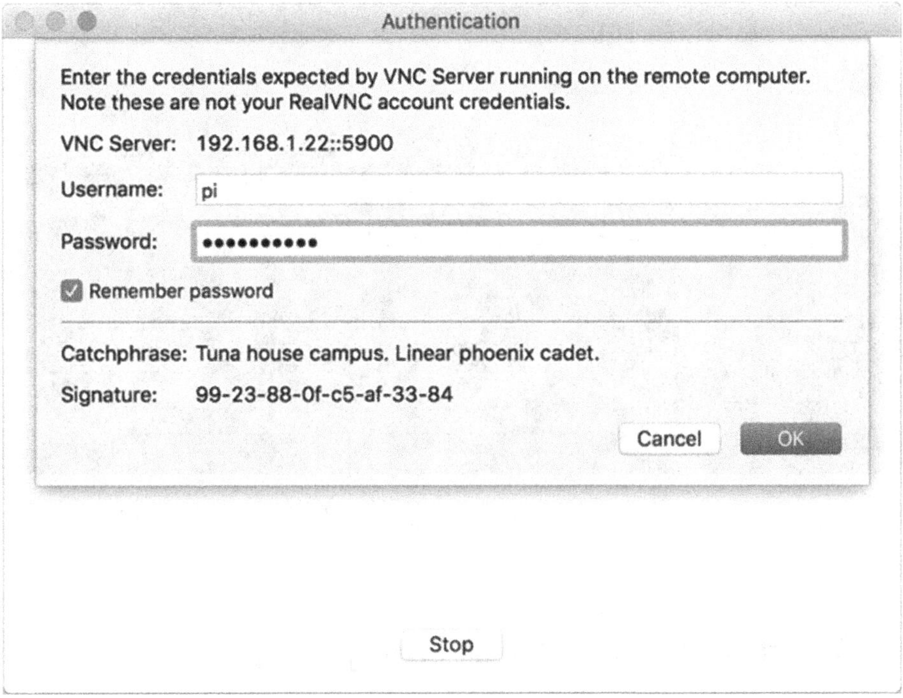

Figure 1-20. *Connecting to the Raspbian desktop via the VNC Viewer*

If this succeeds, you should see the Raspbian desktop. For instance, you can see my Raspbian desktop in Figure 1-21.

Figure 1-21. *Accessing a Raspbian desktop through the VNC Viewer application*

1.10 Powering Off the Raspbian

It's a good idea to turn off your Raspberry Pi when you're not using it. Don't turn off the power directly because doing so can break your board. Instead, you turn off your Raspberry Pi by typing this command on the Terminal.

```
$ sudo shutdown -h -P now
```

After Raspbian shuts down, you'll see the red LED light up. Then unplug the power cable from the board.

If you are working with Raspbian in desktop mode, you can turn off Raspberry Pi by choosing the Shutdown option from the main menu. After you choose this option, you should obtain the dialog shown in Figure 1-22. Click the Shutdown button.

Figure 1-22. *The Shutdown button on the Raspbian desktop*

After the shutdown process is complete, you can unplug the power cable from your Raspberry Pi board.

This is the end of the last session in this chapter.

1.11 Summary

In this chapter, you learned briefly what Raspberry Pi and Raspbian are. You also set up Raspbian on a Raspberry Pi board. Last, you learned how to configure the network and the VNC desktop.

In the next chapter, we focus on the command line in Raspbian. You learn how to operate and manage Raspbian through the Terminal.

CHAPTER 2

The Raspbian OS Command Line

The Raspbian OS provides shells to be used to manage its system. Some shell commands are useful for optimizing your work. In this chapter, you learn how to work with Raspbian shells. You'll see some examples to help you learn and understand the use of the shell.

The following is a list of topics covered in this chapter:

- Understand Raspbian shells

- Work with Raspbian shells

- Manipulate files and directories

- Work with redirection

- Work with resource permissions

- Manipulate processes

- Work with media storage

© Agus Kurniawan 2019
A. Kurniawan, *Raspbian OS Programming with the Raspberry Pi*,
https://doi.org/10.1007/978-1-4842-4212-4_2

2.1 Introducing Raspbian Shells

Raspbian is built from Debian OS. This means that you can operate Raspbian using the Debian/Ubuntu style. In this chapter, you learn about the Raspbian shells, which we usually call the command line.

You can access the Raspbian shell from desktop mode or via remote SSH. If you are working in desktop mode, you can access the Raspbian Terminal by clicking on the Terminal icon. You'll then see the Terminal window, as shown in Figure 2-1.

Figure 2-1. *Accessing the Raspbian Terminal from the desktop*

You also can access the Raspbian Terminal via SSH. For instance, the IP address of Raspbian is 192.168.1.21. You can access remote SSH with the pi account, as follows.

```
$ ssh pi@192.168.1.21
```

If this succeeds, you'll see the Terminal, as shown in Figure 2-2.

Figure 2-2. *Accessing the Raspbian Terminal using remote SSH*

2.2 The Basic Raspbian Shell

In this section, we perform basic shell operations in Raspbian. These shell commands are general commands that you can use in your daily activities.

We explore some basic shells in the following sections.

2.2.1 Rebooting Raspbian OS

Sometimes you'll want to refresh or reload libraries after you've installed or configured something. You'll probably need to reboot your Raspbian. If you want to reboot your Raspberry Pi, use this command:

```
$ sudo shutdown -r now
```

You also can do it by using this command:

```
$ sudo reboot
```

2.2.2 Shutting Down

If you think you won't be using the Raspberry Pi board again, you can turn it off. You should perform a shutdown before unplugging it from the power adapter.

Use this command to perform a shutdown and turn off your Raspberry Pi:

```
$ sudo shutdown -h now
```

Wait several minutes. After that, you can unplug the power cable from the Raspberry Pi board.

2.2.3 Configuring the Timezone

If you want to change the timezone in the Raspberry Pi, you can use the raspi-config tool. You can type this command on the Terminal.

```
$ sudo raspi-config
```

Then, you will get the dialog box shown in Figure 2-3.

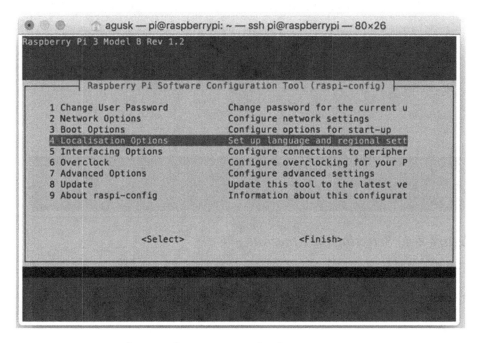

Figure 2-3. *Displaying the raspi-config form*

You can select Localisation Options to configure the timezone. When you're done, you should get the form shown in Figure 2-4.

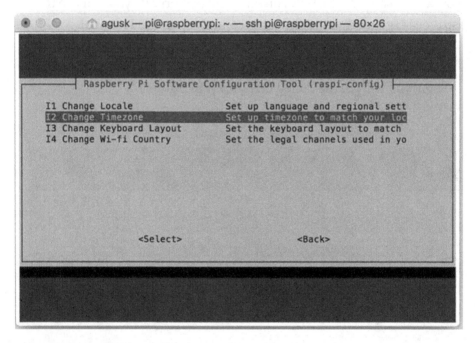

Figure 2-4. *Selecting the timezone*

Then, you select your area to set the timezone. You can see the options in Figure 2-5.

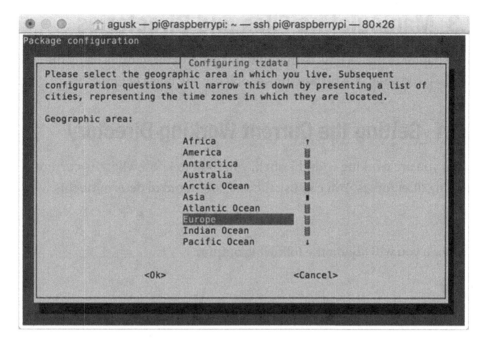

Figure 2-5. *Selecting the appropriate timezone area*

When you're done, your Raspberry Pi will set the timezone that you have selected.

2.2.4 Configuring the Keyboard

You can change the keyboard layout using `raspi-config`. You can follow the instructions from previous section to access the `raspi-config` tool. Select Change Keyboard Layout, which is also shown in Figure 2-4.

Raspbian will detect your keyboard layout automatically.

2.3 Manipulating Files and Directories

This chapter explains how to manipulate files and directories using the Raspberry Pi shell. We explore these topics in the next sections.

2.3.1 Getting the Current Working Directory

When you are working with the shell, you want to know what the current working directory is. You can use the pwd command to determine this.

```
$ pwd
```

Then you will obtain the following output.

```
$ pwd
/home/pi
```

2.3.2 Listing Files and Directories

To list files and directories on the current directory, you can use the ls command.

```
$ ls
```

The sample output is shown in Figure 2-6.

Figure 2-6. *Listing files and directories*

You can change a form in a listing. You can add -l parameter to ls to do this, as follows:

```
$ ls -l
```

The command output is shown in Figure 2-7.

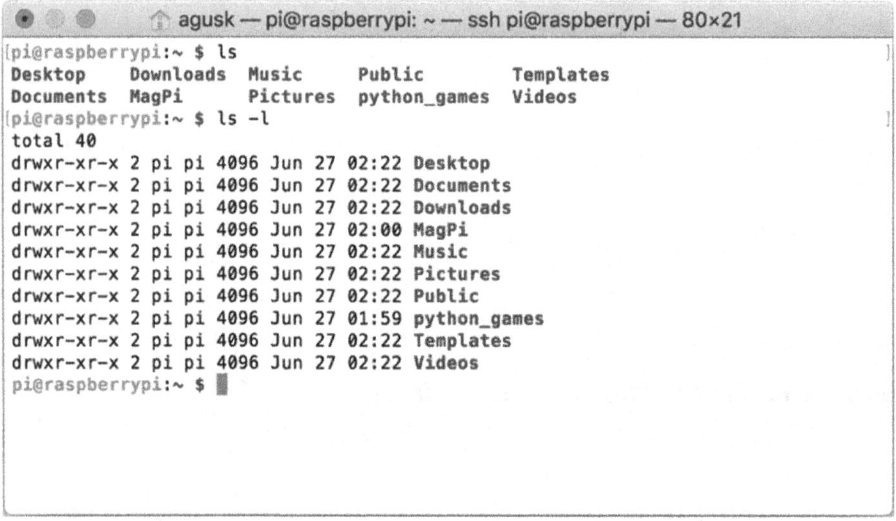

Figure 2-7. *Listing files and directories with the -l parameter*

You can list the contents of a directory using ls as well. For instance, say you want to list the contents of the Documents directory. You would use this command:

```
$ ls Documents/
```

2.3.3 Understanding the ls Parameters

If you want to see the list of parameters used with the ls command, you can call ls with the --help parameter. You can type this command:

```
$ ls --help
```

Then you'll see information about the parameter, as shown in Figure 2-8.

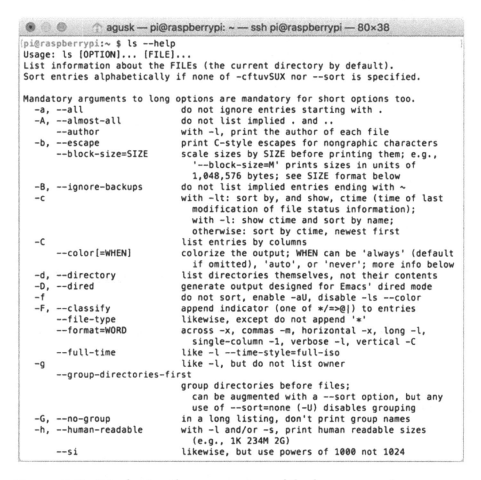

Figure 2-8. *Displaying the parameters of the ls command*

For example, you can use the parameter -l to list the format and -r to reverse the order of the files and directories.

```
$ ls -l -r
```

Sample output can be seen in Figure 2-9.

```
[pi@raspberrypi:~ $ ls -l -r
total 40
drwxr-xr-x 2 pi pi 4096 Jun 27 02:22 Videos
drwxr-xr-x 2 pi pi 4096 Jun 27 02:22 Templates
drwxr-xr-x 2 pi pi 4096 Jun 27 01:59 python_games
drwxr-xr-x 2 pi pi 4096 Jun 27 02:22 Public
drwxr-xr-x 2 pi pi 4096 Jun 27 02:22 Pictures
drwxr-xr-x 2 pi pi 4096 Jun 27 02:22 Music
drwxr-xr-x 2 pi pi 4096 Jun 27 02:00 MagPi
drwxr-xr-x 2 pi pi 4096 Jun 27 02:22 Downloads
drwxr-xr-x 2 pi pi 4096 Jun 27 02:22 Documents
drwxr-xr-x 2 pi pi 4096 Jun 27 02:22 Desktop
pi@raspberrypi:~ $
```

Figure 2-9. Displaying a list of files and directories with the -l and -r parameters

2.3.4 Changing the Current Working Directory

If you want to change the current directory to another directory, you can use the cd command with a parameter that target the directory you want. For instance, say you want to change to the Documents folder. Then you can type this command.

```
$ cd Documents/
```

Sample program output can be seen in Figure 2-10.

```
● ○ ● ⬆ agusk — pi@raspberrypi: ~/Documents — ssh pi@raspberrypi — 80×17
[pi@raspberrypi:~ $ ls -l -r
total 40
drwxr-xr-x 2 pi pi 4096 Jun 27 02:22 Videos
drwxr-xr-x 2 pi pi 4096 Jun 27 02:22 Templates
drwxr-xr-x 2 pi pi 4096 Jun 27 01:59 python_games
drwxr-xr-x 2 pi pi 4096 Jun 27 02:22 Public
drwxr-xr-x 2 pi pi 4096 Jun 27 02:22 Pictures
drwxr-xr-x 2 pi pi 4096 Jun 27 02:22 Music
drwxr-xr-x 2 pi pi 4096 Jun 27 02:00 MagPi
drwxr-xr-x 2 pi pi 4096 Jun 27 02:22 Downloads
drwxr-xr-x 2 pi pi 4096 Jun 27 02:22 Documents
drwxr-xr-x 2 pi pi 4096 Jun 27 02:22 Desktop
[pi@raspberrypi:~ $ cd Documents/
pi@raspberrypi:~/Documents $ █
```

Figure 2-10. *Changing the current directory*

If you don't have any idea as to which directory you want to navigate
to, you can use the Tab key. For instance, say you want to see a list of
directories on the root directory, /. Type this command:

```
$ cd /
```

After that, press the Tab key and then you can see the list of directories. You can see sample output in Figure 2-11.

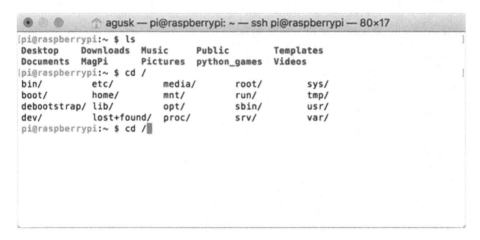

Figure 2-11. *Listing directories using the cd command*

Now type this command.

```
$ cd /usr/
```

Press the Tab key again. You'll see a list of directories under the /usr/ folder. Figure 2-12 shows this command output.

```
[pi@raspberrypi:~ $ ls
Desktop      Downloads  Music      Public        Templates
Documents    MagPi      Pictures   python_games  Videos
[pi@raspberrypi:~ $ cd /
bin/            etc/          media/      root/      sys/
boot/           home/         mnt/        run/       tmp/
debootstrap/    lib/          opt/        sbin/      usr/
dev/            lost+found/   proc/       srv/       var/
[pi@raspberrypi:~ $ cd /usr/
bin/      include/  local/   sbin/    src/
games/    lib/      man/     share/
pi@raspberrypi:~ $ cd /usr/█
```

Figure 2-12. *Listing directories with the cd command on a subfolder*

Sometimes you'll want to go back to the previous directory. You can do this using the cd command with the parameter .. (two dots). Type this command:

```
$ cd ..
```

You'll see the response shown in Figure 2-13.

```
● ● ●           ⌂ agusk — pi@raspberrypi: ~ — ssh pi@raspberrypi — 80×17
[pi@raspberrypi:~ $ ls
Desktop    Downloads  Music      Public         Templates
Documents  MagPi      Pictures   python_games   Videos
[pi@raspberrypi:~ $ cd /
bin/            etc/           media/        root/         sys/
boot/           home/          mnt/          run/          tmp/
debootstrap/    lib/           opt/          sbin/         usr/
dev/            lost+found/    proc/         srv/          var/
[pi@raspberrypi:~ $ cd /usr/
bin/      include/  local/   sbin/    src/
games/    lib/      man/     share/
[pi@raspberrypi:~ $ ls
Desktop    Downloads  Music      Public         Templates
Documents  MagPi      Pictures   python_games   Videos
[pi@raspberrypi:~ $ cd Documents/
[pi@raspberrypi:~/Documents $ cd ..
 pi@raspberrypi:~ $ █
```

Figure 2-13. *Moving back to the previous directory*

2.3.5 Creating a Directory

We can use the mkdir command to create a new directory. For instance, say you want to create a folder called myschool.

```
$ mkdir myschool
```

You can verify that it was created using the ls command. You can then see your newly created directory, as shown in Figure 2-14.

```
agusk — pi@raspberrypi: ~ — ssh pi@raspberrypi — 80×17
[pi@raspberrypi:~ $ ls
Desktop    Downloads  Music      Public           Templates
Documents  MagPi      Pictures   python_games  Videos
[pi@raspberrypi:~ $ mkdir myschool
[pi@raspberrypi:~ $ ls
Desktop    Downloads  Music      Pictures   python_games  Videos
Documents  MagPi      myschool   Public     Templates
pi@raspberrypi:~ $ 
```

Figure 2-14. *Creating a directory*

You also can create multiple directories simultaneously. For instance, you can create these folders—folder1, folder2, and folder3—using the following command:

```
$ mkdir folder1 folder2 folder3
```

Sample program output can be seen in Figure 2-15.

Figure 2-15.   *Creating multiple folders at once*

2.3.6 Removing Files and Directories

To remove a file or directory, you can use the rm command. You can check the rm parameters by typing this command.

```
$ rm --help
```

To delete a file, you specify the filename as the parameter. For instance, say you want to delete the test.txt file. You would type this command to do so.

```
$ rm test.txt
```

You can verify that it was deleted using the ls command. You can see the results in Figure 2-16.

```
● ◎ ●          ⌂ agusk — pi@raspberrypi: ~ — ssh pi@raspberrypi — 80×17
[pi@raspberrypi:~ $ ls                                                        ]
Desktop    Downloads  folder2  MagPi  myschool  Public       Templates  Videos
Documents  folder1    folder3  Music  Pictures  python_games  test.txt
[pi@raspberrypi:~ $ rm test.txt                                               ]
[pi@raspberrypi:~ $ ls                                                        ]
Desktop    Downloads  folder2  MagPi  myschool  Public       Templates
Documents  folder1    folder3  Music  Pictures  python_games  Videos
pi@raspberrypi:~ $ ▓
```

Figure 2-16. *Deleting a file*

If you want to delete a directory, you can use the -rf parameter to force-delete all the content inside the directory.

```
$ rm -rf myschool
```

Then you can check it using the ls command, as shown in Figure 2-17.

```
● ● ●          ⌂ agusk — pi@raspberrypi: ~ — ssh pi@raspberrypi — 80×17
[pi@raspberrypi:~ $ ls
Desktop    Downloads  folder2  MagPi  myschool  Public       Templates
Documents  folder1    folder3  Music  Pictures  python_games  Videos
[pi@raspberrypi:~ $ rm -rf myschool
[pi@raspberrypi:~ $ ls
Desktop    Downloads  folder2  MagPi  Pictures  python_games  Videos
Documents  folder1    folder3  Music  Public    Templates
pi@raspberrypi:~ $ █
```

Figure 2-17. *Deleting files and directories with enforcement*

2.3.7 Copying Files and Directories

You can copy files and directories using the cp command. You can learn about the cp parameters by typing this command.

```
$ cp --help
```

Then you'll obtain the output shown in Figure 2-18.

```
● ● ●           ⬆ agusk — pi@raspberrypi: ~ — ssh pi@raspberrypi — 80×36
pi@raspberrypi:~ $ cp --help
Usage: cp [OPTION]... [-T] SOURCE DEST
  or:  cp [OPTION]... SOURCE... DIRECTORY
  or:  cp [OPTION]... -t DIRECTORY SOURCE...
Copy SOURCE to DEST, or multiple SOURCE(s) to DIRECTORY.

Mandatory arguments to long options are mandatory for short options too.
  -a, --archive              same as -dR --preserve=all
      --attributes-only      don't copy the file data, just the attributes
      --backup[=CONTROL]     make a backup of each existing destination file
  -b                         like --backup but does not accept an argument
      --copy-contents        copy contents of special files when recursive
  -d                         same as --no-dereference --preserve=links
  -f, --force                if an existing destination file cannot be
                               opened, remove it and try again (this option
                               is ignored when the -n option is also used)
  -i, --interactive          prompt before overwrite (overrides a previous -n
                               option)
  -H                         follow command-line symbolic links in SOURCE
  -l, --link                 hard link files instead of copying
  -L, --dereference          always follow symbolic links in SOURCE
  -n, --no-clobber           do not overwrite an existing file (overrides
                               a previous -i option)
  -P, --no-dereference       never follow symbolic links in SOURCE
  -p                         same as --preserve=mode,ownership,timestamps
      --preserve[=ATTR_LIST] preserve the specified attributes (default:
                               mode,ownership,timestamps), if possible
                               additional attributes: context, links, xattr,
                               all
      --no-preserve=ATTR_LIST don't preserve the specified attributes
      --parents              use full source file name under DIRECTORY
  -R, -r, --recursive        copy directories recursively
      --reflink[=WHEN]       control clone/CoW copies. See below
      --remove-destination   remove each existing destination file before
                               attempting to open it (contrast with --force)
      --sparse=WHEN          control creation of sparse files. See below
```

Figure 2-18. *Displaying the cp parameters*

For demo purposes, say you want to copy the test.txt file to the current directory and name it a new name, called test2.txt. If a different text2.txt file exists in that directory, it will be overridden.

```
$ cp test.txt test2.txt
```

The command output can be seen in Figure 2-19.

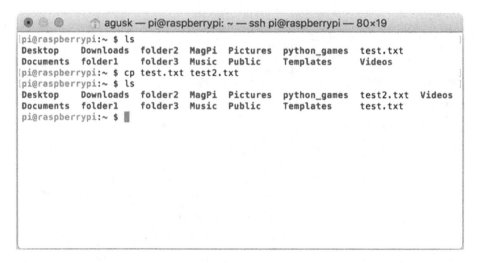

Figure 2-19. *Copying a file*

If you want a confirmation before copying files, use the -i parameter. If the text2.txt file does already exist, you will first be asked if you want to override this file.

```
$ cp -i test.txt test2.txt
```

The command response is shown in Figure 2-20.

```
● ○ ●        ⬆ agusk — pi@raspberrypi: ~ — ssh pi@raspberrypi — 80×19
[pi@raspberrypi:~ $ ls                                                        ]
Desktop     Downloads   folder2  MagPi  Pictures   python_games  test2.txt  Videos
Documents   folder1     folder3  Music  Public     Templates     test.txt
[pi@raspberrypi:~ $ cp -i test.txt test2.txt                                  ]
[cp: overwrite 'test2.txt'? yes                                               ]
[pi@raspberrypi:~ $ ls                                                        ]
Desktop     Downloads   folder2  MagPi  Pictures   python_games  test2.txt  Videos
Documents   folder1     folder3  Music  Public     Templates     test.txt
pi@raspberrypi:~ $ ▌
```

Figure 2-20. *Copying a file with a confirmation*

You can also copy a file into a directory with the same filename. For instance, you can copy the test.txt file to the Documents directory.

```
$ cp test.txt Documents/
```

You also can copy all the files in a directory, including any subdirectories and hidden files/directories, into another directory. For instance, say you want to copy all the files in the Documents directory into the folder1 directory. You would type this command to do this:

```
$ cp -a Documents/ folder1/
```

49

The sample output is shown in Figure 2-21.

```
●  ○  ○        ⌂ agusk — pi@raspberrypi: ~ — ssh pi@raspberrypi — 80×19
[pi@raspberrypi:~ $ ls
Desktop    Downloads  folder2  MagPi  Pictures  python_games  test2.txt  Videos
Documents  folder1    folder3  Music  Public    Templates     test.txt
[pi@raspberrypi:~ $ cp -a Documents/. folder1/
pi@raspberrypi:~ $ █
```

Figure 2-21. *Copying all files and directories into a targeted folder*

2.3.8 Moving Files and Directories

We can move a file or directory to another folder using the mv command. You can also check parameters and usage of the mv command by typing this command.

```
$ mv --help
```

You should see a list of mv parameters. Let's start to work with the mv command.

You can move a file with a new filename, but keep it in the current directory. It basically renaming the file. For instance, say you want to move the test.txt file into current directory with the name mytest.txt. You would use this command:

```
$ mv test.txt mytest.txt
```

You can see the program output in Figure 2-22.

```
● ● ●        ⌂ agusk — pi@raspberrypi: ~ — ssh pi@raspberrypi — 80×19
[pi@raspberrypi:~ $ ls                                                        ]
Desktop    Downloads  folder2 MagPi Pictures  python_games test2.txt Videos
Documents  folder1    folder3 Music Public    Templates    test.txt
[pi@raspberrypi:~ $ mv test.txt mytest.txt                                    ]
[pi@raspberrypi:~ $ ls                                                        ]
Desktop    folder1  MagPi      Pictures      Templates
Documents  folder2  Music      Public        test2.txt
Downloads  folder3  mytest.txt python_games  Videos
pi@raspberrypi:~ $ █
```

Figure 2-22. *Moving a file*

After executing this command, the test.txt file will be removed and a new file, mytest.txt, will be created. If the mytest file exists in the current directory, it will be overridden. You can request a confirmation before mv overrides the file by using the -i parameter.

```
$ mv -i test.txt mytest.txt
```

Now you also can move a file into another folder. For instance, you can move the mytest.txt file into the folder called Documents.

```
$ mv mytest.txt Documents/
```

You can move a folder to another folder, for instance, say you want to move the folder1 folder to folder2. Use this command:

```
$ mv folder1/ folder2/
```

2.3.9 Creating Symbolic Links

You can create a symbolic link using the ln command. You can see how to use this command and view its parameters by typing this command:

```
$ ln --help
```

You'll then see all the ln parameters.

For example, say you want to create a symbolic link called mylink and refer to a file called test2.txt. Use this command sequence:

```
$ ln test2.txt mylink
```

You can see this command program, as shown in Figure 2-23.

```
[pi@raspberrypi:~ $ ls
Desktop     folder1  MagPi       Pictures      Templates
Documents   folder2  Music       Public        test2.txt
Downloads   folder3  mytest.txt  python_games  Videos
[pi@raspberrypi:~ $ ln test2.txt mylink
[pi@raspberrypi:~ $ ls
Desktop     folder1  MagPi       mytest.txt  python_games  Videos
Documents   folder2  Music       Pictures    Templates
Downloads   folder3  mylink      Public      test2.txt
pi@raspberrypi:~ $ ▊
```

Figure 2-23. Creating a symbolic link

If you open File Manager on the Raspbian desktop, you can see the link file, called mylink. Then open this file. You can see the text editor with the test2.txt file.

You also can create a symbolic link for a folder; for instance, you can create a symbolic link called myfolder to the folder folder2/.

```
$ ln -s folder2/ myfolder
```

2.4 Redirection

In this section, we are going to explore how to use redirection on the Raspberry Pi.

2.4.1 Standard Output

Most command-line programs that display their results do so by sending their results to standard output. By default, standard output directs its contents to the display. You can redirect standard output to a file using the > command. For instance, you can call the ls command and then save the result into a file.

```
$ ls > list.txt
```

You can see the list.txt file, which you can open using nano.

```
$ nano list.txt
```

A contents of the list.txt file can be seen in Figure 2-24.

```
[pi@raspberrypi:~ $ ls > list.txt
[pi@raspberrypi:~ $ ls
Desktop     folder1  list.txt  mylink        Public        test2.txt
Documents   folder2  MagPi     mytest.txt    python_games   Videos
Downloads   folder3  Music     Pictures      Templates
pi@raspberrypi:~ $ ▌
```

Figure 2-24. *Redirecting a file*

The > command replaces the existing file. You can append the content using the >> command.

```
$ ls Documents/ >> list.txt
```

2.4.2 Standard Input

By default, standard input gets its contents from the keyboard, but like standard output, it can be redirected. To redirect the standard input to a file instead of to the keyboard, you use the < character. For instance, you can sort data in the list.txt file.

```
$ sort < list.txt
```

The command output is shown in Figure 2-25.

Figure 2-25. *Output from executing a sort*

You can also redirect the result into a new file, called `sorted_list.txt`.

```
$ sort < list.txt > sorted_list.txt
```

2.4.3 Standard Error

You can redirect error to a file using the `2>` command. It can be a program or a Linux command. You can type this command.

```
$ program 2> error.log
$ linux_command 2> error.log
```

You can redirect standard output and error into a file using the following command.

```
$ linux_command &> file
```

2.4.4 Pipelines

You can use I/O redirection to connect multiple commands together with what are called *pipelines*. The following is an example of a pipeline in action:

```
$ ls -l | less
```

The program output can be seen in Figure 2-26.

```
● ● ●              agusk — pi@raspberrypi: ~ — ssh pi@raspberrypi — 80×19
total 68
drwxr-xr-x 2 pi pi 4096 Jun 27 02:22 Desktop
drwxr-xr-x 2 pi pi 4096 Jun 27 02:22 Documents
drwxr-xr-x 2 pi pi 4096 Jun 27 02:22 Downloads
drwxr-xr-x 2 pi pi 4096 Jun 27 02:22 folder1
drwxr-xr-x 2 pi pi 4096 Sep 19 16:06 folder2
drwxr-xr-x 2 pi pi 4096 Sep 19 16:06 folder3
-rw-r--r-- 1 pi pi  147 Sep 19 21:08 list.txt
drwxr-xr-x 2 pi pi 4096 Jun 27 02:00 MagPi
drwxr-xr-x 2 pi pi 4096 Jun 27 02:22 Music
-rw-r--r-- 2 pi pi    7 Sep 19 17:54 mylink
-rw-r--r-- 1 pi pi    7 Sep 19 17:52 mytest.txt
drwxr-xr-x 2 pi pi 4096 Jun 27 02:22 Pictures
drwxr-xr-x 2 pi pi 4096 Jun 27 02:22 Public
drwxr-xr-x 2 pi pi 4096 Jun 27 01:59 python_games
drwxr-xr-x 2 pi pi 4096 Jun 27 02:22 Templates
-rw-r--r-- 2 pi pi    7 Sep 19 17:54 test2.txt
drwxr-xr-x 2 pi pi 4096 Jun 27 02:22 Videos
:
```

Figure 2-26. *Performing a pipeline*

To exit and go back, press the q key on the keyboard.

As another example, you can display the 10 newest files in the current directory:

```
$ ls -lt | head
```

The following is a list of filter parameters you can use on your commands.

- sort
- uniq
- grep
- fmt
- pr
- head
- tail
- tr
- sed
- awk

2.5 Permissions

This section explains how to work with permissions in Raspbian.

2.5.1 Understanding Permissions

First, you can determine our identity information using the `id` command.

```
$ id
```

For instance, you obtain the response shown in Figure 2-27.

```
● ◎ ●        ⌂ agusk — pi@raspberrypi: ~ — ssh pi@raspberrypi — 80×19
[pi@raspberrypi:~ $ id                                                          ]
uid=1000(pi) gid=1000(pi) groups=1000(pi),4(adm),20(dialout),24(cdrom),27(sudo),
29(audio),44(video),46(plugdev),60(games),100(users),101(input),108(netdev),997(
gpio),998(i2c),999(spi)
pi@raspberrypi:~ $ ▊
```

Figure 2-27. *Output from the id command*

Now you can evaluate permissions on each file or directory. You can pass the -l parameter on ls to display permissions.

```
$ ls -l
```

The program output is shown in Figure 2-28.

```
● ● ●        🏠 agusk — pi@raspberrypi: ~ — ssh pi@raspberrypi — 80×24
[pi@raspberrypi:~ $ id
uid=1000(pi) gid=1000(pi) groups=1000(pi),4(adm),20(dialout),24(cdrom),27(sudo),
29(audio),44(video),46(plugdev),60(games),100(users),101(input),108(netdev),997(
gpio),998(i2c),999(spi)
[pi@raspberrypi:~ $ ls -l
total 68
drwxr-xr-x 2 pi pi 4096 Jun 27 02:22 Desktop
drwxr-xr-x 2 pi pi 4096 Jun 27 02:22 Documents
drwxr-xr-x 2 pi pi 4096 Jun 27 02:22 Downloads
drwxr-xr-x 2 pi pi 4096 Jun 27 02:22 folder1
drwxr-xr-x 2 pi pi 4096 Sep 19 16:06 folder2
drwxr-xr-x 2 pi pi 4096 Sep 19 16:06 folder3
-rw-r--r-- 1 pi pi  147 Sep 19 21:08 list.txt
drwxr-xr-x 2 pi pi 4096 Jun 27 02:00 MagPi
drwxr-xr-x 2 pi pi 4096 Jun 27 02:22 Music
-rw-r--r-- 2 pi pi    7 Sep 19 17:54 mylink
-rw-r--r-- 1 pi pi    7 Sep 19 17:52 mytest.txt
drwxr-xr-x 2 pi pi 4096 Jun 27 02:22 Pictures
drwxr-xr-x 2 pi pi 4096 Jun 27 02:22 Public
drwxr-xr-x 2 pi pi 4096 Jun 27 01:59 python_games
drwxr-xr-x 2 pi pi 4096 Jun 27 02:22 Templates
-rw-r--r-- 2 pi pi    7 Sep 19 17:54 test2.txt
drwxr-xr-x 2 pi pi 4096 Jun 27 02:22 Videos
pi@raspberrypi:~ $ ▇
```

Figure 2-28. *Listing permission on an ls command*

Note these two commands from Figure 2-28:

```
drwxr-xr-x 2 pi pi 4096 Jun  27 02:22 Documents
-rw-r--r-- 2 pi pi    7 Sep  19 17:54 test2.txt
```

Let's explore the `drwxr-xr-x` command in more detail. See Figure 2-29.

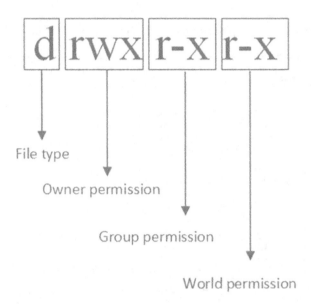

Figure 2-29. *Permission information*

The following is a list of file types:

```
d ----> directory
- -------> regular file
l ----> symbolic link
c ---> character special file
b ---> block special file
```

The following is a list of permission attributes:

```
r ---> read permission
w ---> write permission
x ---> execute permission
- ---> no permission
```

Now we go back to the permission drwxr-xr-x. You know that it's a folder. The owner has read, write, and execute permissions. The group has read and execute permissions. The rest have read and execute permissions.

2.5.2 chmod

The chmod command is used to change permissions on a file or directory. We can use chmod with the octal representation or symbolic representation.

The octal representation for permissions is constructed as follows:

- The first number is for the user

- The second number is for the group

- The third number is for all others

For instance, if you wanted to give read and write permissions (6) to the user and read permissions (4) to the group and others, you would use the following command:

```
$ chmod 644 filename
```

Note:

- The 6 octal number converts to the binary number: 110. This means 110 is rw-

- The 4 octal number converts to the binary number: 100. This means 100 is r--

As another example, say you want to give read and execute permissions (5) to the user, read permissions (4) to the group, and nothing (0) to the others. You would use the following command:

```
$ chmod 540 filename
```

Note:

- The 5 octal number converts to the binary number: 111. This means 110 is `rwx`

- The 4 octal number converts to the binary number: 100. This means 100 is `r--`

- The 0 octal number converts to the binary number: 000. This means 000 is `---` (no permissions)

The second way that you can change permissions is by applying the symbolic representation. Following is a list of the symbolic representations:

- `u` is for user

- `g` is for group

- `o` is for others

For instance, you can add execute permissions (using the + symbol) to the user with this command.

```
$ chmod u+x filename
```

If you also can add multiple permissions for users and groups.

```
$ chmod u+r,g+x filename
```

To remove permissions, you use the - symbol. For instance, you can remove read and execute permissions from a file by using this command.

```
$ chmod u-rx filename
```

Use the -R option to change the permission recursively. Here is an example command.

```
$ chmod -R 755 my-directory/
```

2.5.3 chown

The chown command is used to change the user and/or group ownership of a given file. The following syntax is for chown.

```
$ chown owner-user file
$ chown owner-user:owner-group file
$ chown owner-user:owner-group directory
$ chown options owner-user:owner-group file
```

For instance, say you want to obtain permissions for the test.log file.

```
$ ls -l test.log
```

The following is the result.

```
$ -rw-r--r-- 1 pi pi   837 Feb  4 06:19 test.log
```

You can see the file owner is now pi.
Now you change ownership of the test.log file.

```
$ chown agusk test.log
```

Try to display the permissions again on the test.log file, use this command:

```
$ -rw-r--r-- 1 agusk pi   837 Feb  4 06:19 test.log
```

You also can change the ownership and group related to a file.

```
$ chown agusk:agusk test.log
```

You can see the permissions of the test.log file as follows.

```
$ -rw-r--r-- 1 agusk agusk   837 Feb  4 06:19 test.log
```

2.6 Manipulating Processes

In this section, we explore how to work with processes in Raspbian. To view processes, you can use the following commands:

- ps

- top

Each command will be explained in the following sections.

2.6.1 ps

The ps command can be used to view the current processes, including their process identification numbers (PIDs). Simply type ps on the Terminal.

```
$ ps
```

You'll see the current process, as shown in Figure 2-30.

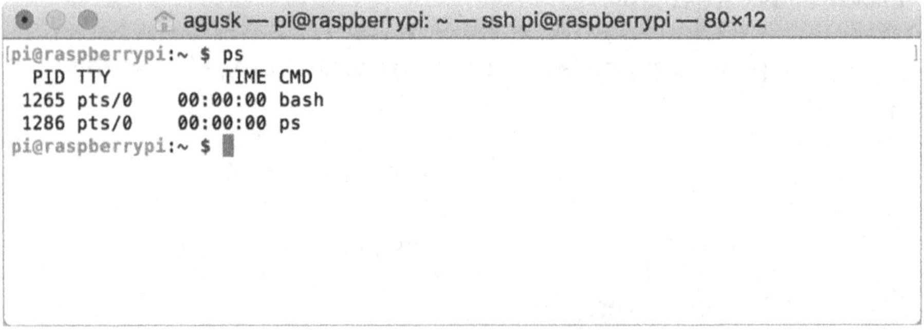

Figure 2-30. *A list of current processes in Raspbian*

If you want to know details about the current process, you can pass the x parameter with the ps command.

```
$ ps x
```

The command output is shown in Figure 2-31.

```
●  ○  ●        ⌂ agusk — pi@raspberrypi: ~ — ssh pi@raspberrypi — 80×29
[pi@raspberrypi:~ $ ps x                                                      ]
  PID TTY      STAT    TIME COMMAND
  605 ?        Ss      0:00 /lib/systemd/systemd --user
  608 ?        S       0:00 (sd-pam)
  613 ?        Ssl     0:00 /usr/bin/lxsession -s LXDE-pi -e LXDE
  622 ?        Ss      0:00 /usr/bin/dbus-daemon --session --address=systemd: --n
  748 ?        Ss      0:00 /usr/bin/ssh-agent x-session-manager
  765 tty1     S+      0:00 -bash
  770 ?        Ssl     0:00 /usr/lib/gvfs/gvfsd
  779 ?        Sl      0:00 /usr/lib/gvfs/gvfsd-fuse /run/user/1000/gvfs -f -o bi
  806 ?        S       0:00 openbox --config-file /home/pi/.config/openbox/lxde-p
  809 ?        Sl      0:00 lxpolkit
  810 ?        Sl      0:03 lxpanel --profile LXDE-pi
  811 ?        Sl      0:01 pcmanfm --desktop --profile LXDE-pi
  820 ?        Ss      0:00 /usr/bin/ssh-agent -s
  845 ?        Ssl     0:00 /usr/lib/menu-cache/menu-cached /run/user/1000/menu-c
  849 ?        Ssl     0:00 /usr/lib/gvfs/gvfs-udisks2-volume-monitor
  862 ?        Z       0:00 [sh] <defunct>
  869 ?        Ssl     0:00 /usr/lib/gvfs/gvfs-afc-volume-monitor
  874 ?        Ssl     0:00 /usr/lib/gvfs/gvfs-gphoto2-volume-monitor
  878 ?        Ssl     0:00 /usr/lib/gvfs/gvfs-goa-volume-monitor
  882 ?        Ssl     0:00 /usr/lib/gvfs/gvfs-mtp-volume-monitor
  918 ?        Sl      0:00 /usr/lib/gvfs/gvfsd-trash --spawner :1.4 /org/gtk/gvf
 1046 ?        S       0:00 /usr/bin/vncserverui service 15
 1061 ?        S       0:00 /usr/bin/vncserverui -statusicon 7
 1262 ?        S       0:00 sshd: pi@pts/0
 1265 pts/0    Ss      0:00 -bash
 1287 pts/0    R+      0:00 ps x
pi@raspberrypi:~ $ ▊
```

Figure 2-31. *A list of current processes using ps with the x parameter*

Note the symbols in the STAT column in Figure 2-31. This information can be found in the document. The following is a list of process states:

- D: Uninterruptible sleep (usually IO)

- R: Running or runnable (on run queue)

- S: Interruptible sleep (waiting for an event to complete)

- **T**: Stopped, either by a job control signal or because it is being traced

- W: Paging (not valid since the 2.6.xx kernel)

- X: Dead (should never be seen)

- Z: Defunct ("zombie") process, terminated but not reaped by its parent

If you want to know more information about the current process, you can use the following command.

```
$ ps -aux | less
```

Note:

- Parameter -a displays all processes.

- Parameter -u tells the ps command to provide detailed information about each process.

- Parameter -x adds to the list processes that have no controlling terminal, for instance daemons.

The sample output is shown in Figure 2-32. Press q to exit the ps application.

```
● ● ●        ⌂ agusk — pi@raspberrypi: ~ — ssh pi@raspberrypi — 80×29
USER        PID %CPU %MEM    VSZ   RSS TTY       STAT START    TIME COMMAND
root          1  0.1  0.6  27056  6072 ?          Ss  06:35    0:01 /sbin/init spla
sh
root          2  0.0  0.0      0     0 ?           S  06:35    0:00 [kthreadd]
root          4  0.0  0.0      0     0 ?          I<  06:35    0:00 [kworker/0:0H]
root          6  0.0  0.0      0     0 ?          I<  06:35    0:00 [mm_percpu_wq]
root          7  0.0  0.0      0     0 ?           S  06:35    0:00 [ksoftirqd/0]
root          8  0.0  0.0      0     0 ?           I  06:35    0:00 [rcu_sched]
root          9  0.0  0.0      0     0 ?           I  06:35    0:00 [rcu_bh]
root         10  0.0  0.0      0     0 ?           S  06:35    0:00 [migration/0]
root         11  0.0  0.0      0     0 ?           S  06:35    0:00 [cpuhp/0]
root         12  0.0  0.0      0     0 ?           S  06:35    0:00 [cpuhp/1]
root         13  0.0  0.0      0     0 ?           S  06:35    0:00 [migration/1]
root         14  0.0  0.0      0     0 ?           S  06:35    0:00 [ksoftirqd/1]
root         16  0.0  0.0      0     0 ?          I<  06:35    0:00 [kworker/1:0H]
root         17  0.0  0.0      0     0 ?           S  06:35    0:00 [cpuhp/2]
root         18  0.0  0.0      0     0 ?           S  06:35    0:00 [migration/2]
root         19  0.0  0.0      0     0 ?           S  06:35    0:00 [ksoftirqd/2]
root         21  0.0  0.0      0     0 ?          I<  06:35    0:00 [kworker/2:0H]
root         22  0.0  0.0      0     0 ?           S  06:35    0:00 [cpuhp/3]
root         23  0.0  0.0      0     0 ?           S  06:35    0:00 [migration/3]
root         24  0.0  0.0      0     0 ?           S  06:35    0:00 [ksoftirqd/3]
root         25  0.0  0.0      0     0 ?           I  06:35    0:00 [kworker/3:0]
root         26  0.0  0.0      0     0 ?          I<  06:35    0:00 [kworker/3:0H]
root         27  0.0  0.0      0     0 ?           S  06:35    0:00 [kdevtmpfs]
root         28  0.0  0.0      0     0 ?          I<  06:35    0:00 [netns]
root         32  0.0  0.0      0     0 ?           I  06:35    0:00 [kworker/3:1]
root         33  0.0  0.0      0     0 ?           S  06:35    0:00 [khungtaskd]
:█
```

Figure 2-32. *Listing processes with the -aux parameter*

As another option, you can use the following command.

```
$ ps -ef | less
```

You can view processes in tree form. You can also use the pstree command.

```
$ pstree | less
```

You can see this command output in Figure 2-33. Press q to exit the ps application.

```
● ◉ ●        ⌂ agusk — pi@raspberrypi: ~ — ssh pi@raspberrypi — 80×29
systemd-+-avahi-daemon---avahi-daemon
        |-bluealsa-+-{bactl}
        |          |-{gdbus}
        |          `-{gmain}
        |-bluetoothd
        |-cron
        |-dbus-daemon
        |-dhcpcd
        |-hciattach
        |-lightdm-+-Xorg-+-{InputThread}
        |        |      |-{llvmpipe-0}
        |        |      |-{llvmpipe-1}
        |        |      |-{llvmpipe-2}
        |        |      `-{llvmpipe-3}
        |        |-lightdm-+-lxsession-+-lxpanel-+-sh
        |        |        |           |         |      |-{gdbus}
        |        |        |           |         |      |-{gmain}
        |        |        |           |         |      `-{menu-cache-io}
        |        |        |           |         |-lxpolkit-+-{gdbus}
        |        |        |           |         |          `-{gmain}
        |        |        |           |         |-openbox
        |        |        |           |         |-pcmanfm-+-{gdbus}
        |        |        |           |         |         `-{gmain}
        |        |        |           |         |-ssh-agent
        |        |        |           |         |-{gdbus}
        |        |        |           |         `-{gmain}
        |        |        |-{gdbus}
        |        |        `-{gmain}
:█
```

Figure 2-33. *Listing processes in tree form*

2.6.2 top

The top command displays the processes in order of CPU usage. You can type this command.

```
$ top
```

After it's executed, you'll see a list of processes to CPU usage, as shown in Figure 2-34.

```
● ● ●          ⬆ agusk — pi@raspberrypi: ~ — ssh pi@raspberrypi — 80×29
top - 06:54:59 up 19 min,  3 users,  load average: 0.00, 0.00, 0.00
Tasks: 122 total,   1 running,  79 sleeping,   0 stopped,   1 zombie
%Cpu(s):  0.2 us,  0.2 sy,  0.0 ni, 99.6 id,  0.0 wa,  0.0 hi,  0.0 si,  0.0 st
KiB Mem :  949452 total,   663812 free,    84732 used,   200908 buff/cache
KiB Swap:  102396 total,   102396 free,        0 used.   798640 avail Mem

  PID USER      PR  NI    VIRT    RES    SHR S  %CPU %MEM     TIME+ COMMAND
 1294 pi        20   0    8108   3288   2824 R   1.0  0.3   0:00.11 top
  810 pi        20   0  140780  24548  19976 S   0.3  2.6   0:03.48 lxpanel
    1 root      20   0   27056   6072   4892 S   0.0  0.6   0:01.90 systemd
    2 root      20   0       0      0      0 S   0.0  0.0   0:00.00 kthreadd
    4 root       0 -20       0      0      0 I   0.0  0.0   0:00.00 kworker/0:+
    6 root       0 -20       0      0      0 I   0.0  0.0   0:00.00 mm_percpu_+
    7 root      20   0       0      0      0 S   0.0  0.0   0:00.00 ksoftirqd/0
    8 root      20   0       0      0      0 I   0.0  0.0   0:00.11 rcu_sched
    9 root      20   0       0      0      0 I   0.0  0.0   0:00.00 rcu_bh
   10 root      rt   0       0      0      0 S   0.0  0.0   0:00.00 migration/0
   11 root      20   0       0      0      0 S   0.0  0.0   0:00.00 cpuhp/0
   12 root      20   0       0      0      0 S   0.0  0.0   0:00.00 cpuhp/1
   13 root      rt   0       0      0      0 S   0.0  0.0   0:00.00 migration/1
   14 root      20   0       0      0      0 S   0.0  0.0   0:00.03 ksoftirqd/1
   16 root       0 -20       0      0      0 I   0.0  0.0   0:00.00 kworker/1:+
   17 root      20   0       0      0      0 S   0.0  0.0   0:00.00 cpuhp/2
   18 root      rt   0       0      0      0 S   0.0  0.0   0:00.00 migration/2
   19 root      20   0       0      0      0 S   0.0  0.0   0:00.00 ksoftirqd/2
   21 root       0 -20       0      0      0 I   0.0  0.0   0:00.00 kworker/2:+
   22 root      20   0       0      0      0 S   0.0  0.0   0:00.00 cpuhp/3
   23 root      rt   0       0      0      0 S   0.0  0.0   0:00.00 migration/3
   24 root      20   0       0      0      0 S   0.0  0.0   0:00.01 ksoftirqd/3
```

Figure 2-34. *Displaying processes to CPU usage*

Press M to display the processes sorted by memory usage. If you want to exit, press q.

We can specify the data by user as well. For instance, you use this command if you want to display processes by the user called pi.

```
$ top -u pi
```

You can see this command output in Figure 2-35.

```
● ● ●          ⬆ agusk — pi@raspberrypi: ~ — ssh pi@raspberrypi — 80×29
top - 06:56:01 up 20 min,  3 users,  load average: 0.00, 0.00, 0.00
Tasks: 122 total,   1 running,  79 sleeping,   0 stopped,   1 zombie
%Cpu(s):  0.2 us,  0.2 sy,  0.0 ni, 99.5 id,  0.0 wa,  0.0 hi,  0.0 si,  0.0 st
KiB Mem :   949452 total,   663812 free,    84712 used,   200928 buff/cache
KiB Swap:   102396 total,   102396 free,        0 used.   798660 avail Mem

  PID USER      PR  NI    VIRT    RES    SHR S  %CPU %MEM     TIME+ COMMAND
 1332 pi        20   0    8108   3292   2824 R   1.3  0.3   0:00.18 top
  810 pi        20   0  140904  24588  19976 S   0.7  2.6   0:03.63 lxpanel
  605 pi        20   0    9664   5812   5068 S   0.0  0.6   0:00.14 systemd
  608 pi        20   0   11312   1352     88 S   0.0  0.1   0:00.00 (sd-pam)
  613 pi        20   0   52504  12564  11300 S   0.0  1.3   0:00.23 lxsession
  622 pi        20   0    6508   3560   3144 S   0.0  0.4   0:00.10 dbus-daemon
  748 pi        20   0    3796    228     16 S   0.0  0.0   0:00.00 ssh-agent
  765 pi        20   0    6176   4044   2752 S   0.0  0.4   0:00.30 bash
  770 pi        20   0   39652   5860   5312 S   0.0  0.6   0:00.06 gvfsd
  779 pi        20   0   56484   6304   5656 S   0.0  0.7   0:00.05 gvfsd-fuse
  806 pi        20   0   52728  13596  11692 S   0.0  1.4   0:00.28 openbox
  809 pi        20   0   43100  11012   9988 S   0.0  1.2   0:00.06 lxpolkit
  811 pi        20   0  110484  23084  19776 S   0.0  2.4   0:01.10 pcmanfm
  820 pi        20   0    3796    228     16 S   0.0  0.0   0:00.00 ssh-agent
  845 pi        20   0   28444   6236   5732 S   0.0  0.7   0:00.04 menu-cached
  849 pi        20   0   74528  10136   9064 S   0.0  1.1   0:00.10 gvfs-udisk+
  862 pi        20   0       0      0      0 Z   0.0  0.0   0:00.00 sh
  869 pi        20   0   50968   5028   4436 S   0.0  0.5   0:00.03 gvfs-afc-v+
  874 pi        20   0   38836   4936   4424 S   0.0  0.5   0:00.03 gvfs-gphot+
  878 pi        20   0   37344   4404   4072 S   0.0  0.5   0:00.02 gvfs-goa-v+
  882 pi        20   0   37264   4528   4104 S   0.0  0.5   0:00.02 gvfs-mtp-v+
  918 pi        20   0   51340   7880   7088 S   0.0  0.8   0:00.08 gvfsd-trash
```

Figure 2-35. *Displaying processes by username*

2.6.3 Killing Processes

Sometimes you'll want to stop processes by killing them. To stop a process, you can use the kill command. You must know the process ID (PID), which you can determine via the ps command. For instance, say you want to stop a process with PID 2093. You would type the following command.

```
$ kill 2093
```

If you have a security problem, you can add the sudo command.

```
$ sudo kill 2093
```

To verify whether the process has stopped, you can use the ps command with the -ef parameter.

```
$ ps -ef
```

We can also stop all processes related to a particular name using the killall command. Here is the basic syntax:

```
$ killall [options] program_name
```

For instance, say you want to stop all processes related to Java. In that case, you would use this command:

```
$ killall java
```

2.6.4 Viewing Memory

We can view unused and used memory and swap space using the free command. Just type this command:

```
$ free
```

The sample output is shown in Figure 2-36.

```
[pi@raspberrypi:~ $ free
               total        used        free      shared  buff/cache   available
Mem:          949452       84628      663492       15700      201332      798740
Swap:         102396           0      102396
pi@raspberrypi:~ $
```

Figure 2-36. *Displaying a list of free memory*

71

2.7 Media Storage

In this section, I'm going to explain how to work with media storage.

2.7.1 Displaying Free Disk Space

To show the statistics about the amount of free disk space you have on the specified file system, you use the df command as follows:

```
$ df -h
```

A sample of the output can be seen in Figure 2-37.

```
● ◎ ●          🏠 agusk — pi@raspberrypi: ~ — ssh pi@raspberrypi — 80×14
[pi@raspberrypi:~ $ df -h
Filesystem      Size  Used Avail Use% Mounted on
/dev/root        15G  4.0G  9.9G  29% /
devtmpfs        460M     0  460M   0% /dev
tmpfs           464M     0  464M   0% /dev/shm
tmpfs           464M   13M  452M   3% /run
tmpfs           5.0M  4.0K  5.0M   1% /run/lock
tmpfs           464M     0  464M   0% /sys/fs/cgroup
/dev/mmcblk0p1   43M   22M   21M  51% /boot
tmpfs            93M     0   93M   0% /run/user/1000
pi@raspberrypi:~ $ ▊
```

Figure 2-37. *Displaying free disk space*

You can display the total hard disk space, including any removable disks. You must type the following command as the root user:

```
$ sudo fdisk -l | grep Disk
```

You can see my sample output in Figure 2-38.

```
[pi@raspberrypi:~ $ sudo fdisk -l | grep Disk
Disk /dev/ram0: 4 MiB, 4194304 bytes, 8192 sectors
Disk /dev/ram1: 4 MiB, 4194304 bytes, 8192 sectors
Disk /dev/ram2: 4 MiB, 4194304 bytes, 8192 sectors
Disk /dev/ram3: 4 MiB, 4194304 bytes, 8192 sectors
Disk /dev/ram4: 4 MiB, 4194304 bytes, 8192 sectors
Disk /dev/ram5: 4 MiB, 4194304 bytes, 8192 sectors
Disk /dev/ram6: 4 MiB, 4194304 bytes, 8192 sectors
Disk /dev/ram7: 4 MiB, 4194304 bytes, 8192 sectors
Disk /dev/ram8: 4 MiB, 4194304 bytes, 8192 sectors
Disk /dev/ram9: 4 MiB, 4194304 bytes, 8192 sectors
Disk /dev/ram10: 4 MiB, 4194304 bytes, 8192 sectors
Disk /dev/ram11: 4 MiB, 4194304 bytes, 8192 sectors
Disk /dev/ram12: 4 MiB, 4194304 bytes, 8192 sectors
Disk /dev/ram13: 4 MiB, 4194304 bytes, 8192 sectors
Disk /dev/ram14: 4 MiB, 4194304 bytes, 8192 sectors
Disk /dev/ram15: 4 MiB, 4194304 bytes, 8192 sectors
Disk /dev/mmcblk0: 14.9 GiB, 15931539456 bytes, 31116288 sectors
Disklabel type: dos
Disk identifier: 0x388194d1
pi@raspberrypi:~ $
```

Figure 2-38. Displaying all total hard disk space

2.7.2 mount

The mount command mounts a storage device or filesystem, making it accessible and attaching it to an existing directory structure. To view all mounted external devices, use the mount command.

```
$ mount
```

The command output can be seen in Figure 2-39.

```
[pi@raspberrypi:~ $ mount
/dev/mmcblk0p2 on / type ext4 (rw,noatime,data=ordered)
devtmpfs on /dev type devtmpfs (rw,relatime,size=470116k,nr_inodes=117529,mode=7
55)
sysfs on /sys type sysfs (rw,nosuid,nodev,noexec,relatime)
proc on /proc type proc (rw,relatime)
tmpfs on /dev/shm type tmpfs (rw,nosuid,nodev)
devpts on /dev/pts type devpts (rw,nosuid,noexec,relatime,gid=5,mode=620,ptmxmod
e=000)
tmpfs on /run type tmpfs (rw,nosuid,nodev,mode=755)
tmpfs on /run/lock type tmpfs (rw,nosuid,nodev,noexec,relatime,size=5120k)
tmpfs on /sys/fs/cgroup type tmpfs (ro,nosuid,nodev,noexec,mode=755)
cgroup on /sys/fs/cgroup/systemd type cgroup (rw,nosuid,nodev,noexec,relatime,xa
ttr,release_agent=/lib/systemd/systemd-cgroups-agent,name=systemd)
cgroup on /sys/fs/cgroup/cpuset type cgroup (rw,nosuid,nodev,noexec,relatime,cpu
set)
cgroup on /sys/fs/cgroup/cpu,cpuacct type cgroup (rw,nosuid,nodev,noexec,relatim
e,cpu,cpuacct)
cgroup on /sys/fs/cgroup/freezer type cgroup (rw,nosuid,nodev,noexec,relatime,fr
eezer)
cgroup on /sys/fs/cgroup/net_cls type cgroup (rw,nosuid,nodev,noexec,relatime,ne
```

Figure 2-39. *Performing the mount command*

If you have a flashdisk, you can plug it into your Raspberry Pi via a USB. Normally this device will appear as /dev/sda1.

```
$ ls /dev/sda*
```

This command output is shown in Figure 2-40.

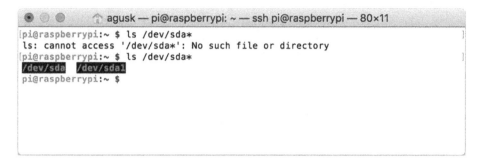

Figure 2-40. *Listing all external flashdisks*

Now how do you mount this device? First, you create a directory on /
media/, for instance myfd. Type this command to do so:

$ sudo mkdir /media/myfd

Then you can mount your flashdisk using the following command:

$ sudo mount -o uid=pi,gid=pi /dev/sda1 /media/myfd

You may obtain the warning, "mount: warning: /media/myfd seems
to be mounted read-only.". I used a flashdisk with the NTFS format. To
solve this warning, install the ntfs-3g package.

$ sudo apt-get install ntfs-3g

If your flashdisk has the exfat format, you can install the following
libraries.

$ sudo apt-get install exfat-fuse exfat-utils

Now try to mount the flashdisk using this command:

$ sudo mount -o uid=pi,gid=pi /dev/sda1 /media/myfd

You can see there is no warning. You can see my command output in Figure 2-41.

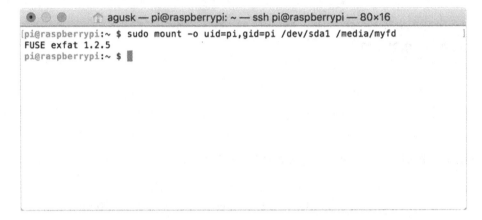

Figure 2-41. *Mounting a flashdisk*

You can then check the result by listing the contents of the flashdisk using the ls command.

```
$ ls /media/myfd
```

You can see the output in Figure 2-42.

```
●  ●  ●          ⌂ agusk — pi@raspberrypi: ~ — ssh pi@raspberrypi — 80×16
[pi@raspberrypi:~ $ sudo mount -o uid=pi,gid=pi /dev/sda1 /media/myfd        ]
 FUSE exfat 1.2.5
[pi@raspberrypi:~ $ ls /media/myfd                                           ]
 DL-CUDA.mp4  phd  System Volume Information
 pi@raspberrypi:~ $ █
```

Figure 2-42. *Listing all contents from the flashdisk*

2.7.3 umount

The umount command "unmounts" a mounted filesystem. It tells the system to complete any pending read or write operations and then safely detaches the filesystem.

For instance, say you want to remove the flashdisk on /media/myfd. You type this command.

```
$ sudo umount /media/myfd
```

2.8 Summary

You learned how to work with the Raspbian shell, from basic uses, to using processes, working with storage, and manipulating permissions.

In the next chapter, we focus on the Raspbian program. You learn how to build programs using the Raspbian OS.

CHAPTER 3

Programming on Raspbian OS

Raspbian OS provides application tools to write programs. In this chapter, you learn to write programs on Raspbian. Then, you'll learn how to execute the program.

The following is a list of topics that you learn about in this chapter:

- Understand the programming model in Raspbian
- Set up the programming environment
- Write Python programs
- Write Node.js programs
- Write C/C++ programs

3.1 Understand the Programming Model in Raspbian OS

Raspberry Pi with Raspbian OS is a complete development environment for programming. You can develop programs in Raspbian in three ways:

- Desktop mode
- Terminal mode on desktop mode
- Terminal mode over remote SSH

© Agus Kurniawan 2019
A. Kurniawan, *Raspbian OS Programming with the Raspberry Pi*,
https://doi.org/10.1007/978-1-4842-4212-4_3

Desktop mode is easier to start to build programs on Raspbian. You just need a monitor, a keyboard, and a mouse to write programs. Some programming tools are provided by Raspbian. You can see these tools in Figure 3-1.

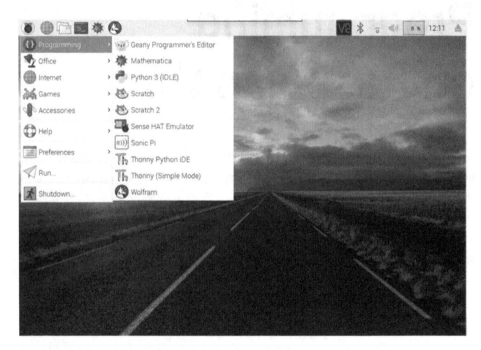

Figure 3-1. *Programming tools on the Raspbian desktop*

The Raspbian desktop also provides office tools to write document and manage spreadsheets. You can see them in Figure 3-2.

Figure 3-2. *Office tools on the Raspbian desktop*

You can also write programs on the Raspbian Terminal. You can run, write, and execute them. You can see my checking Python version in Figure 3-3.

Figure 3-3. *Writing programs using the Terminal from the desktop mode*

Last, you can write programs on the Raspbian Terminal over remote SSH. You can see my remote SSH Python access in Figure 3-4.

```
● ○ ●        ⌂ agusk — pi@raspberrypi: ~ — ssh pi@raspberrypi — 80×16
[pi@raspberrypi:~ $ python -V                                                ]
Python 2.7.13
[pi@raspberrypi:~ $ python3 -V                                               ]
Python 3.5.3
pi@raspberrypi:~ $ ▐
```

Figure 3-4. *Accessing Python from a remote SSH*

3.2 Setting Up the Programming Environment

In general, we don't have to put more effort into the Raspberry Pi board and Raspbian OS to set up programming. By default, Python 2.7.x and 3.5.x have Raspbian Scratch desktop edition installed.

We explore Raspbian programming on Python, Node.js, and C/C++ in the next sections.

3.3 Python Programming

Most people use Python to write programs on a Raspberry Pi board. There are many libraries and frameworks for Python. You can read and review the Python project officially at https://www.python.org.

In this section, we review some ways to write programs on Raspbian.

3.3.1 Python 3 (IDLE)

If you prefer to work in desktop mode, Raspbian provides Python 3 (IDLE) to develop a Python program in Raspbian. You can find it on the Programming menu. From there, you should get the Python shell, as shown in Figure 3-5.

Figure 3-5. *The Python 3.5.3 shell*

For demo purposes, write the following scripts.

```
>>> a = 3
>>> b = 5
>>> c = a * b
>>> print(c)
```

A sample of the program output can be seen in Figure 3-6.

Figure 3-6. *Executing Python on a shell*

3.3.2 Thonny Python IDE

Thonny is a Python IDE used to develop Python programs. You can write Python scripts and save those into Python files. Thonny also provides a running tool so you can see the program output from an IDE. The Thonny project can be found at `https://thonny.org`.

The Thonny IDE is installed in the Raspbian Scratch desktop by default. You can find it on the Programming menu. From there, you can see the form shown in Figure 3-7.

Now you can write Python program as follows.

```
a = 10
b = 3
c = a * b
print(c)
```

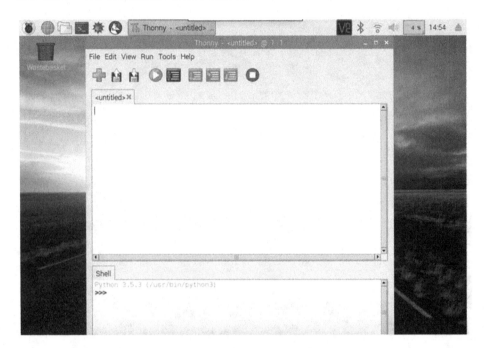

Figure 3-7. *Thonny Python IDE application*

Save this program into a file called `simple.py`, by clicking the array-disk icon with a down arrow. See Figure 3-8.

Figure 3-8. *Writing programs on the Thonny application*

Now you can run this file by clicking the green arrow, as shown in Figure 3-9. When you are done, you should see the program output at the bottom of the IDE.

Figure 3-9. *Executing a program on the Thonny application*

3.3.3 Python Shell from Remote SSH

You can write a Python program via remote SSH. After you're connected, you can use the nano tool to write the program.

```
$ nano hello.py
```

You will get a form of nano, as shown in Figure 3-10.

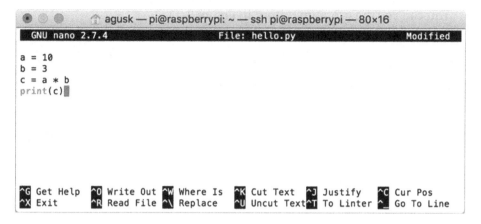

Figure 3-10. Writing Python scripts on the nano application

You can write these scripts:

```
a = 10
b = 3
c = a * b
print(c)
```

Save these scripts. Then, you can run this file.

```
$ python hello.py
```

You can see the program output in Figure 3-11.

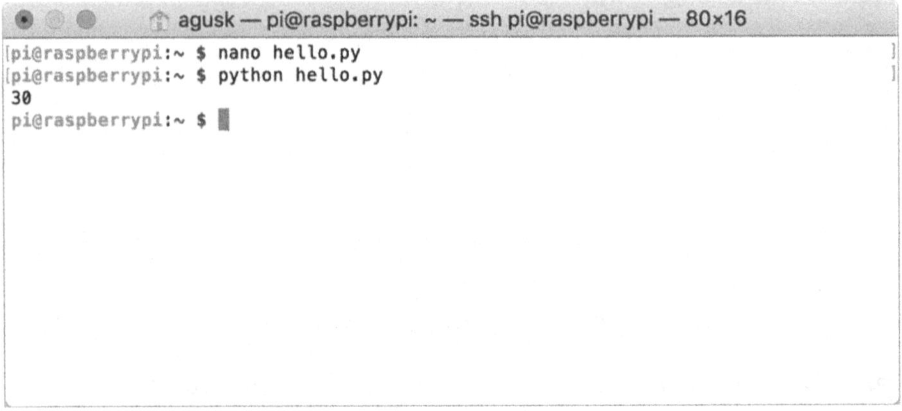

Figure 3-11. *Executing a Python file on the Terminal*

3.3.4 What's Next?

There are many resources to learn Python programming. You can find resources from books and online websites. You can also learn more about Python from the official documentation at `https://docs.python.org/3/`.

3.4 Node.js Programming

Node.js is an open source server environment. Node.js runs on various platforms, such as Windows, Linux, UNIX, and Mac OSX. Node.js adopts JavaScript as its programming language. Officially, the Node.js project can be found at `https://nodejs.org/`.

The Raspbian Scratch desktop version is installed. In this section, we will install Node.js from the Node.js website. First, you need to check the MCU edition. Type this command to do so.

```
$ uname -a
```

You should see your MCU edition. For instance, the Raspberry Pi 3 board uses ARMv7, as shown in Figure 3-12.

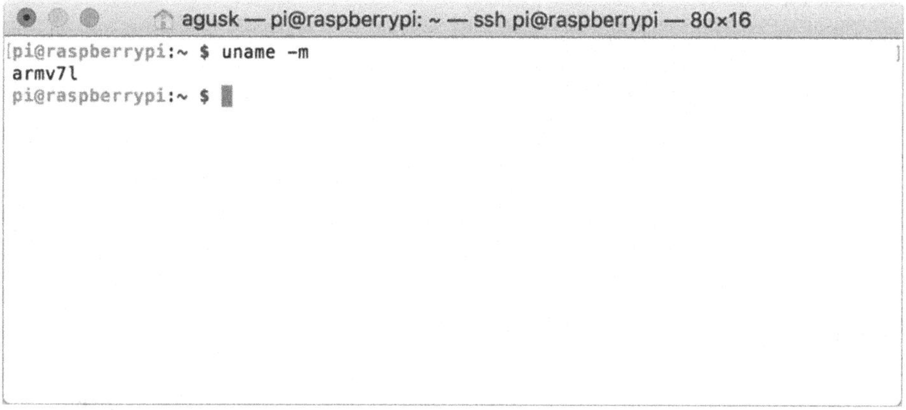

Figure 3-12. *Checking the MCU edition*

You can download Node.js for your MCU platform based on previous checking at `https://nodejs.org/en/download/`.

In these examples, we use Node.js v8.12.0. You can download and extract it by typing this command.

```
$ wget https://nodejs.org/dist/v8.12.0/node-v8.12.0-linux-
armv7l.tar.gz
$ tar -xzf node-v8.12.0-linux-armv7l.tar.gz
```

Program output can be seen in Figure 3-13. Then, you can configure it. Type these commands to do so.

```
$ cd node-v8.12.0-linux-armv7l/
$ sudo cp -R * /usr/local/
```

```
● ● ●        ⬆ agusk — pi@raspberrypi: ~ — ssh pi@raspberrypi — 80×16
--2018-09-20 16:29:45--  https://nodejs.org/dist/v8.12.0/node-v8.12.0-linux-armv
7l.tar.gz
Resolving nodejs.org (nodejs.org)... 104.20.23.46, 104.20.22.46, 2400:cb00:2048:
1::6814:172e, ...
Connecting to nodejs.org (nodejs.org)|104.20.23.46|:443... connected.
HTTP request sent, awaiting response... 200 OK
Length: 16204404 (15M) [application/gzip]
Saving to: 'node-v8.12.0-linux-armv7l.tar.gz'

node-v8.12.0-linux- 100%[====================>]  15.45M  1.71MB/s    in 9.1s

2018-09-20 16:29:55 (1.69 MB/s) - 'node-v8.12.0-linux-armv7l.tar.gz' saved [1620
4404/16204404]

[pi@raspberrypi:~ $ tar -xzf node-v8.12.0-linux-armv7l.tar.gz
pi@raspberrypi:~ $ ▮
```

Figure 3-13. *Download and extract the Node.js application*

After that, you can check if the download was successful by typing these commands.

```
$ node -v
$ npm -v
```

If these commands succeeded, you should see the Node.js and NPM versions, as shown in Figure 3-14.

```
● ● ●  ⬆ agusk — pi@raspberrypi: ~/node-v8.12.0-linux-armv7l — ssh pi@raspberrypi...
Length: 16204404 (15M) [application/gzip]
Saving to: 'node-v8.12.0-linux-armv7l.tar.gz'

node-v8.12.0-linux- 100%[====================>]  15.45M  1.71MB/s    in 9.1s

2018-09-20 16:29:55 (1.69 MB/s) - 'node-v8.12.0-linux-armv7l.tar.gz' saved [1620
4404/16204404]

[pi@raspberrypi:~ $ tar -xzf node-v8.12.0-linux-armv7l.tar.gz              ]
[pi@raspberrypi:~ $ cd node-v8.12.0-linux-armv7l/                         ]
[pi@raspberrypi:~/node-v8.12.0-linux-armv7l $ sudo cp -R * /usr/local/     ]
[pi@raspberrypi:~/node-v8.12.0-linux-armv7l $ node -v                      ]
v8.12.0
[pi@raspberrypi:~/node-v8.12.0-linux-armv7l $ npm -v                       ]
6.4.1
pi@raspberrypi:~/node-v8.12.0-linux-armv7l $ ▮
```

Figure 3-14. *Checking the Node.js and NPM versions*

Now you'll write a simple Node.js application. You can use the nano
application to do so.

```
$ node hello.js
```

Then, write the script shown in Figure 3-15.

```
console.log("hello node.js");
```

Figure 3-15. *Writing a Node.js program*

When you're done, run this program.

```
$ node hello.js
```

You should see messages on the Terminal. Figure 3-16 is a sample of
the typical program output.

```
[pi@raspberrypi:~ $ nano hello.js
[pi@raspberrypi:~ $ node hello.js
hello node.js
pi@raspberrypi:~ $ █
```

Figure 3-16. Running the Node.js application

3.5 C/C++ Programming

GCC is installed in Raspbian by default. This means you can write programs for C/C++. You can verify this by typing this command:

```
$ gcc--version
```

You should see the GCC version, as shown in Figure 3-17.

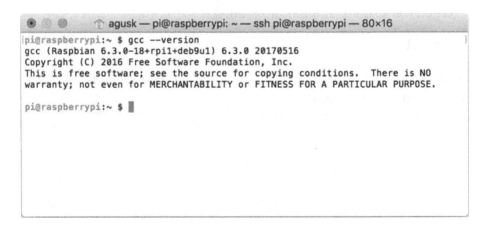

```
[pi@raspberrypi:~ $ gcc --version
gcc (Raspbian 6.3.0-18+rpi1+deb9u1) 6.3.0 20170516
Copyright (C) 2016 Free Software Foundation, Inc.
This is free software; see the source for copying conditions.  There is NO
warranty; not even for MERCHANTABILITY or FITNESS FOR A PARTICULAR PURPOSE.

pi@raspberrypi:~ $ █
```

Figure 3-17. Checking the GCC version

For demo purposes, let's create a simple code example, called `hello world`. Create this file:

```
$ nano hello.c
```

Then, you can write this program. You can see it in Figure 3-18.

```c
#include<stdio.h>

int main()
{
    printf("Hello World\r\n");
    return 0;

}
```

Save this program.

Figure 3-18. *Writing a simple C program*

Now you compile and run this program by typing these commands.

```
$ gcc hello.c -o hello
$ ./hello
```

If the commands succeed, you should see program output shown in Figure 3-19.

```
●  ○  ○          ⬆ agusk — pi@raspberrypi: ~ — ssh pi@raspberrypi — 80×16
[pi@raspberrypi:~ $ gcc --version                                           ]
gcc (Raspbian 6.3.0-18+rpi1+deb9u1) 6.3.0 20170516
Copyright (C) 2016 Free Software Foundation, Inc.
This is free software; see the source for copying conditions.  There is NO
warranty; not even for MERCHANTABILITY or FITNESS FOR A PARTICULAR PURPOSE.

[pi@raspberrypi:~ $ nano hello.c                                            ]
[pi@raspberrypi:~ $ gcc hello.c -o hello                                    ]
[pi@raspberrypi:~ $ ./hello                                                 ]
Hello World
pi@raspberrypi:~ $ ▊
```

Figure 3-19. *Compiling and running the C program*

3.6 Summary

In this chapter, you learned how to develop programs in Python, Node.js, and C/C++. It's a good idea to practice more in these areas by developing programs with various use cases.

The next chapter, you learn all about the Wolfram Language and Mathematica on a Raspberry Pi board with Raspbian OS.

CHAPTER 4

Computational Mathematics with the Wolfram Language and Mathematica

The Wolfram Language and Mathematica are exclusive tools and libraries of the Raspbian OS on the Raspberry Pi board. In this chapter, we explore the Wolfram Language and Mathematica from a programming view.

The following is a list of topics covered in this chapter:

- Understand the Wolfram Language and Mathematica

- Set up Wolfram and Mathematica

- Develop a Hello World program

- Learn basic programming for Wolfram and Mathematica

- Learn computational mathematics with Wolfram and Mathematica

© Agus Kurniawan 2019
A. Kurniawan, *Raspbian OS Programming with the Raspberry Pi*,
https://doi.org/10.1007/978-1-4842-4212-4_4

4.1 Introducing Wolfram Language and Mathematica

Wolfram Language and Mathematica are available for the Raspberry Pi board and come bundled with the Raspbian operating system. Programs can be run from a Pi command line or as a background process, as well as through a notebook interface on the Pi or on a remote computer. On the Pi, the Wolfram Language supports direct programmatic access to standard Pi ports and devices. For further information about this project, you can visit http://www.wolfram.com/raspberry-pi/.

After you have deployed Raspbian on Raspberry Pi, you can run Raspbian in GUI mode and then you should see the Wolfram and Mathematica icons. You can see these icons in Figure 4-1.

Figure 4-1. *The Wolfram and Mathematica icons on the Raspbian bar*

You also find these application icons in the main menu, as shown in Figure 4-2.

Figure 4-2. *The Wolfram and Mathematica menu options on the Raspbian main menu*

The Wolfram application has a Terminal form to run programs. If you execute the Wolfram application, you should see the Terminal application, as shown in Figure 4-3.

Figure 4-3. *Running the Wolfram application from the Terminal*

Otherwise, you can execute the Mathematica application. Then, you get the form shown in Figure 4-4.

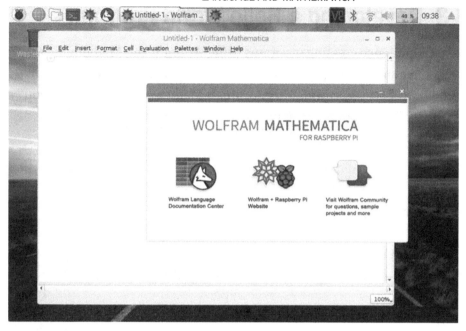

Figure 4-4. *Running the Mathematica application*

Next, we learn how these tools work with computation mathematics.

4.2 Setting Up Wolfram and Mathematica

Technically, we don't discuss setting up Wolfram and Mathematica
in any more detail. If you download and deploy the latest Raspbian
on the Raspberry Pi boards, you will get free licenses for Wolfram and
Mathematica.

In the next section, we create a simple program on Wolfram and
Mathematica.

4.3 Developing a Hello World Program

To get experience creating programs using Wolfram and Mathematica, we
will build a simple program, using a simple mathematics operation. For
demo purposes, you can click the Wolfram Mathematica icon. Then, you
get the Wolfram Mathematica Editor, shown in Figure 4-5.

Now type these scripts:

```
a = 3
b = 5
c = a * b
```

Figure 4-5. *Running programs on Mathematica*

To run these scripts, press Shift+Enter (press the Shift and Enter keys
together) and you'll obtain the resulting output. Sample output can be
seen in Figure 4-5.

You also can run the same scripts in the Wolfram Terminal. You can
type the script line-by-line. Then, you will get response directly. Sample
program output from the Wolfram Terminal can be seen in Figure 4-6.

Figure 4-6. *Running programs from the Wolfram Terminal*

4.4 Basic Programming

In this section, you learn how to write programs for Wolfram and the
Mathematica language. You learn the essential programming language
steps from Wolfram and Mathematica.

You can follow the guidelines in the next sections.

4.4.1 Data Types and Declaring Variables

You can declare a variable and assign a value using the = syntax. If you
don't want to assign a value to a variable, you can set . as the value. You
also can use := to delay assignment.

On a notebook from the Mathematica Editor, you can type these
scripts:

```
a =.
b = 3
c := 5
str = "hello world"
```

Run these scripts by pressing the Shift+Enter keys. You can see the
program output in Figure 4-7.

Figure 4-7. *Declaring variables*

4.4.2 Arithmetic Operators

Mathematica has arithmetic operators that you can use to manipulate numbers. The following is a list of its arithmetic operators:

- + addition

- - subtraction

- * multiplication

- / division

- ^ exponentiation

For demo purposes, write these scripts.

```
m = 8
n = 5

p = m + n
p = m - n
p = m * n
p = m / n
p = m^2
```

The sample program output is shown in Figure 4-8.

Figure 4-8. *Program output for arithmetic operators*

4.4.3 Relational and Logical Operators

We can perform logical operations in Mathematica as well. The following is a list of logical operators:

- < less than

- > greater than

- <= less than or equal

- >= greater than or equal

- == equal to

- != not equal to

- || or

- ! not

- && and

- xor[a,b] exclusive or

For further information, I recommend you read the Wolfram and Mathematica documentation, `https://reference.wolfram.com/ language/tutorial/RelationalAndLogicalOperators.html`.

For demo purposes, we examine logical operators. Write the following scripts.

```
m = 10
n = 5

m < n
m <= n
m > n
m >= n
m == n
m != n
(m < n) && (m > 10)
(m <= 2) || (n > 2)
```

You can see this program output in Figure 4-9.

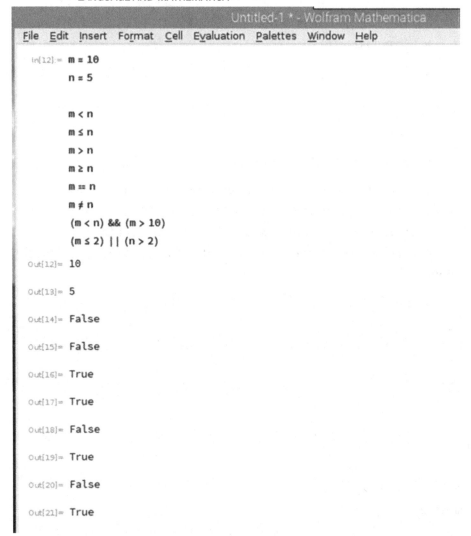

Figure 4-9. *Program output for logical operations*

4.4.4 Conditional Statements

Sometimes we want to manipulate data with a conditional.

In Mathematica, we can use the if and switch statements. We explore these statements in the next sections.

4.4.4.1 if

We can write a Mathematica script for conditional statements, using the
If[] statement. The following is general statement of if[].

```
If[statement,do if true, do if false]
```

Let's write this example:

```
x = 3;
y = 0;
If[x > 1, y = Sqrt[x], y = x^2];
Print[y]
m := If[x > 5, 1, 0];
Print[m]
```

You can type this program into Mathematica and you will get the
program output shown in Figure 4-10.

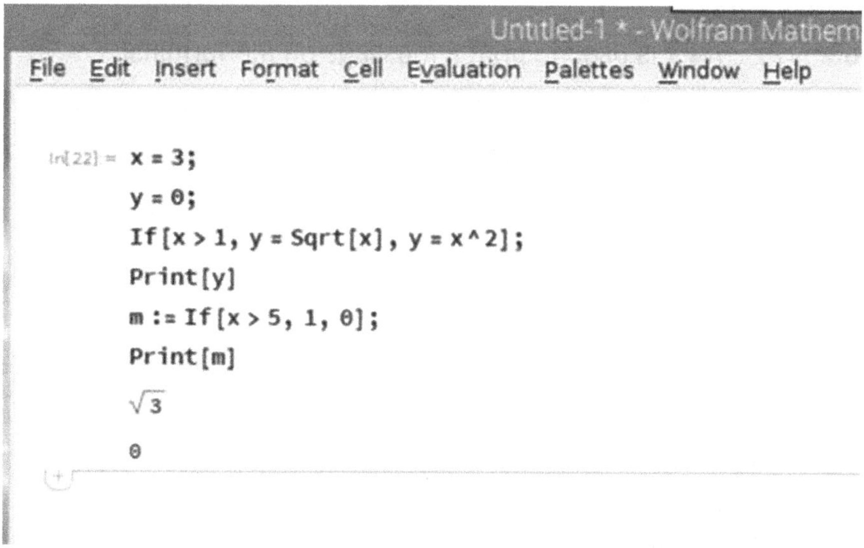

Figure 4-10. *Program output from an if application*

4.4.4.2 **switch**

You can select one of several options in Mathematica. You can use the Switch[] statement. Switch[] can be defined as follows:

Switch[statement, case 1, do case 1 ...., case n,do case n, _ , do default case]

A sample Switch[] script can be written as follows:

```
k = 2;
n = 0;
Switch[k, 1, n = k + 10, 2, n = k^2 + 3, _, n = -1];
Print[n]

k = 5;
n := Switch[k, 1, k + 10, 2, k^2 + 3, _, -1];
Print[n]
```

Note   Print[] is used to print a message on the Terminal.

Run the program. You will get the program output that is shown in Figure 4-11.

```
Untitled-1 * - Wolfram Mathematica

File  Edit  Insert  Format  Cell  Evaluation  Palettes  Window  Help

In[28] = k = 2;
        n = 0;
        Switch[k, 1, n = k + 10, 2, n = k^2 + 3, _, n = -1];
        Print[n]


        k = 5;
        n := Switch[k, 1, k + 10, 2, k^2 + 3, _, -1];
        Print[n]

        7

        -1
```

Figure 4-11. *Program output sample for Switch[]*

4.4.5 Looping

If you perform continuous tasks, it's wise to use a looping scenario to get
those tasks done. In Mathematica, you can perform looping using the
following statements:

- do statements
- for statements
- while statements

Each type of looping statement will be reviewed in the next sections.

4.4.5.1 Do

The first looping statement is the Do[ ] statement. The Do[ ] statement can
be defined as follows:

Do[do_something, {index}]

index is the amount of looping.

For instance, if you want to print "Hello Mathematica" five times, you would write this script.

```
Do[Print["Hello Mathematica"], {5}]
```

Run the program in Mathematica. If you do so, you'll get the response shown in Figure 4-12.

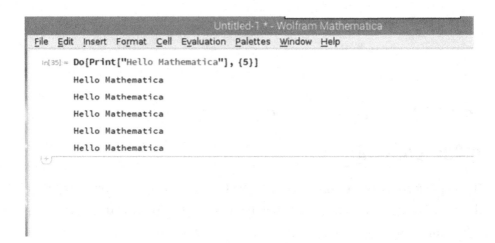

Figure 4-12. *Program output for a do statement*

You also can include an index number in the looping statement. You can write this script for example:

```
Do[Print["counter ", i], {i, 5}]
```

After it's executed, you'll see the output shown in Figure 4-13.

```
                              Untitled-1 * - Wolfram Mathematica
File   Edit   Insert   Format   Cell   Evaluation   Palettes   Window   Help


In[36]:=  Do[Print["counter ", i], {i, 5}]

          counter 1

          counter 2

          counter 3

          counter 4

          counter 5
```

Figure 4-13. *Displaying an index on a looping program*

4.4.5.2 For

If you have experience with C/C++, you can use a for statement in the
same way. The For[] statement in Mathematica is defined as follows:

For[initial,conditional, increment/decrement, do_something]

For testing purposes, you can print a message five times. Write this
script.

For[i = 0, i < 5, i++, Print["index ", i]]

Run the script and you'll see the program output shown in Figure 4-14.

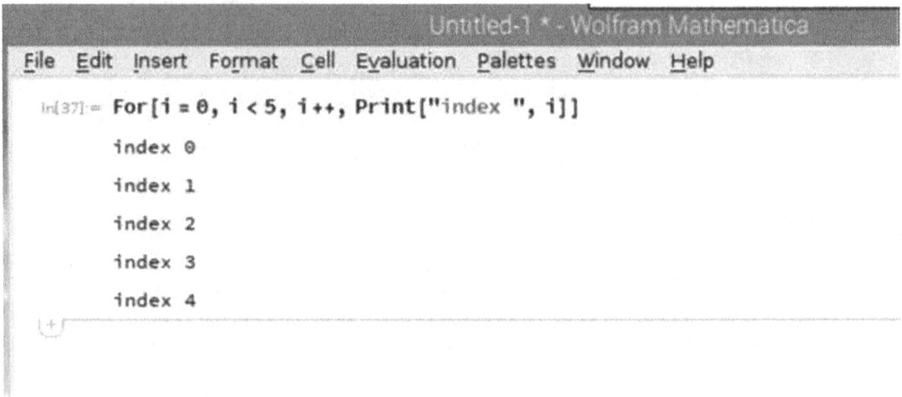

```
In[37]:= For[i = 0, i < 5, i++, Print["index ", i]]

         index 0

         index 1

         index 2

         index 3

         index 4
```

Figure 4-14. *A looping program with For[]*

4.4.5.3 While

The last looping statement that we can use in Mathematica is While[].
This statement can be defined as follows:

```
While[conditional, do_something]
```

For demo purposes, write this script:

```
j = 0;
While[j < 5, Print["j=", j]; j++;]
```

This will print value 0 through value 4. You can see the program output
in Figure 4-15.

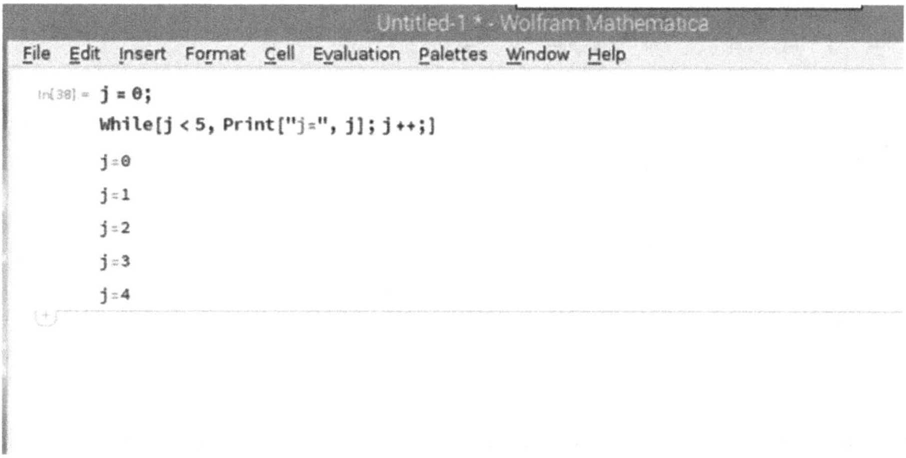

Figure 4-15. *Looping program written with While[]*

4.4.5.4 Break and Continue

Break[] is used to exit the nearest enclosing loop. Continue[] is used to go to the next step in the current loop. Try writing these scripts for demo purposes:

```
For[i = 0, i < 10, i++,
 Print[i];
 If[i == 2, Continue[]];
 If[i == 5, Break[]]
]
```

The program will stop a moment when the value of i is 2. The program also stops on value i = 5. You can see the program output in Figure 4-16.

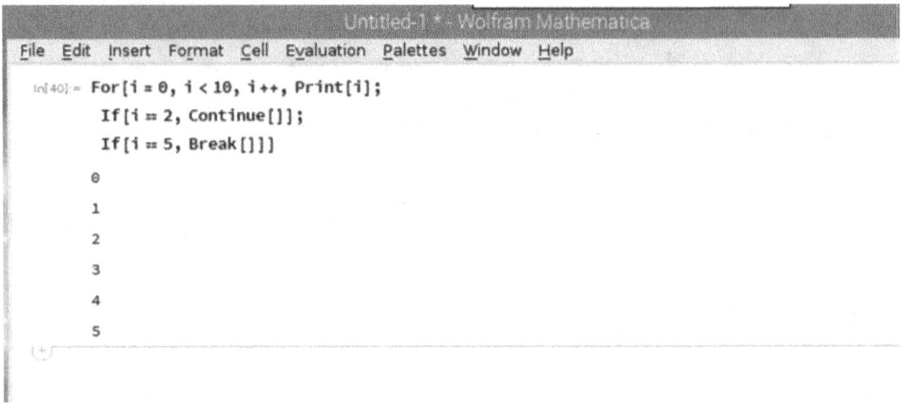

Figure 4-16. *Program demo using Break[] and Continue[]*

4.4.6 Adding Comments

To add comments to your code, which is a very good idea, you can use the (* *) characters. You should use comments in your scripts, which the application will not run, to explain what certain lines of code and scripts are meant to do. Figure 4-17 shows comments added to scripts.

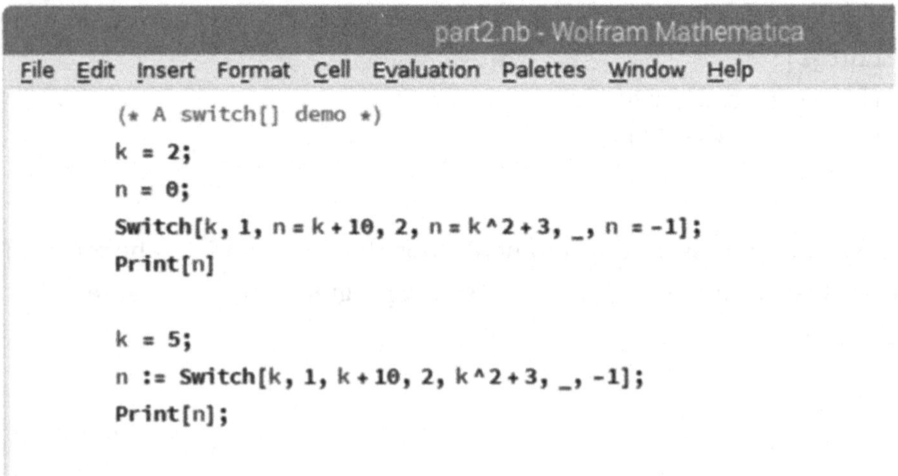

Figure 4-17. *Adding comments to scripts*

4.4.7 Functions

If you have scripts that are called continuously, consider using functions to avoid redundant scripts. You can wrap them into a function. A function in Mathematica can be defined as follows:

```
function[params_] := do_something
```

For testing purposes, we define a simple Mathematics function as follows:

```
Clear[f, x, y];
f[x_] := (x - 2) * Sqrt[x];
Print[f[15]];
Print[f[8]];
```

You should get the program output shown in Figure 4-18 when you execute these scripts.

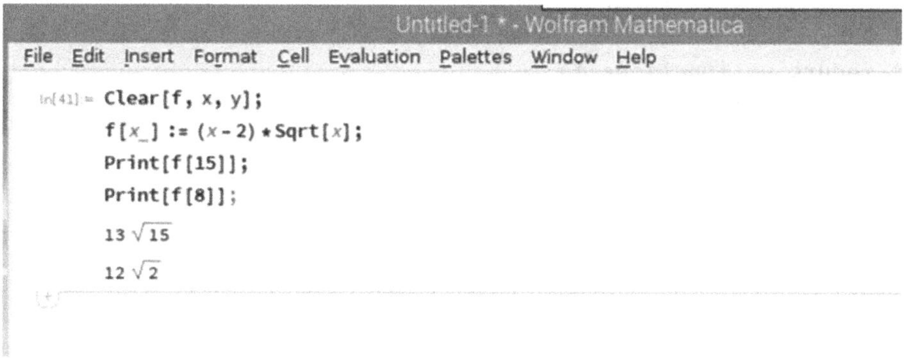

Figure 4-18. *A function in Mathematica*

In a function, you can define parameters as input. You can also add two parameters or more. For instance, you can write these scripts.

```
Clear[f, x, y];
f[x_, y_] := x^2 + y;
```

117

```
Print[f[5, 8]];
Print[f[2, 3]];
```

The program output of these scripts can be seen in Figure 4-19.

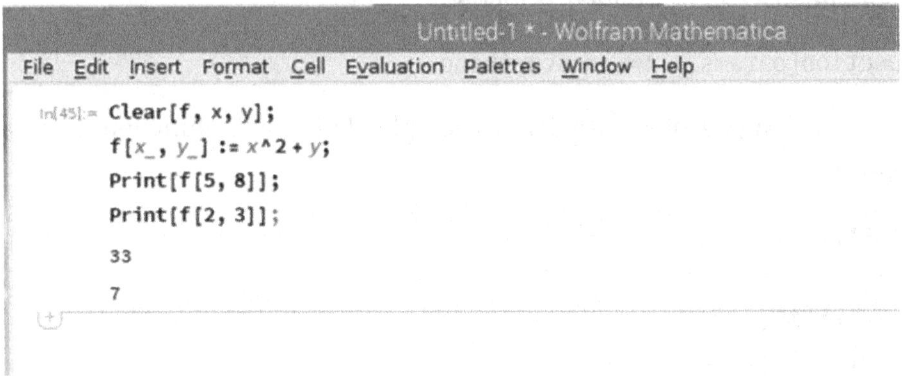

Figure 4-19. *A function with parameters*

You can implement a recursive function in Mathematica as well. For instance, you can write these scripts:

```
(* recursive functions *)
ClearAll[h, n];
h[0] = 10;
h[n_] := 0.58 * h[n - 1];
Print[h[10]];
```

Now you can run this program. Figure 4-20 shows the program output sample.

```
In[49]:= (*recursive functions*)
        ClearAll[h, n];
        h[0] = 10;
        h[n_] := 0.58*h[n-1];
        Print[h[10]];

        0.0430804
```

Figure 4-20. *A sample of a recursive function*

4.5 Computational Mathematics

This chapter explains how to work with computational mathematics using Mathematica. We will discuss several mathematics problems as follows:

- Calculus

- Matrix

- Quadratic equations

- Linear equations

Let's go.

4.5.1 Calculus

There are many topics in calculus. In this section, we focus on plotting an equation, defining limits, performing differentiation, performing integration, and summing.

We explore these topics in the next sections.

4.5.1.1 Plot

We can use Plot[] to display a graph. You can read more about this function at https://reference.wolfram.com/language/ref/Plot.html.

For demo purposes, we create two equations as follows.

$$f_1 = \cos x$$
$$f_2 = x^2 - 2\sin x$$

On Mathematica, we can implement this as follows.

```
Plot[Cos[x], {x, 0, 3 Pi}]
Plot[x^2 - 2 Sin[x], {x, 0, 3 Pi}]
```

You can see the program output in Figure 4-21.

Furthermore, try some more examples. Plot the following equations.

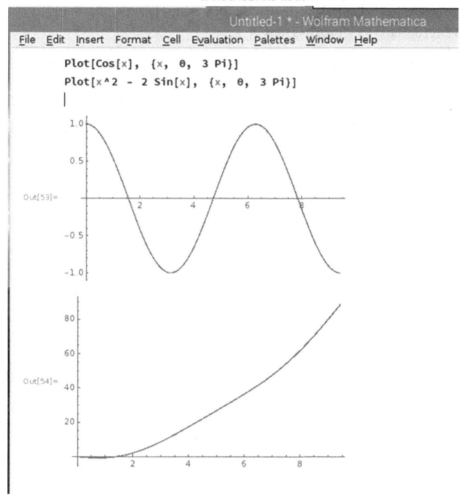

Figure 4-21. *Plotting math equations*

$$f_1 = \sin x$$
$$f_2 = \cos x$$
$$f_3 = 0.1x - 1$$
$$f_4 = 0.5\sin x$$

Those equations can be implemented in Mathematica as follows.

```
Plot[{Sin[x], Cos[x], 0.1 x - 1, 0.5 Sin[x]}, {x, 0, 6 Pi},
 PlotLegends -> "Expressions"]
```

The program output from those scripts can be seen in Figure 4-22.

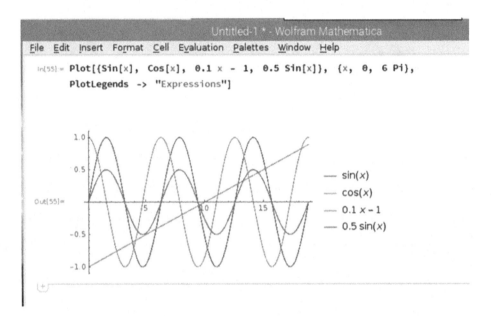

Figure 4-22. *Plotting the sin and cos equations*

4.5.1.2 Limits

We can implement limits in Mathematica using the `Limit[]` syntax. For more information about this statement, check it out at `https://reference.wolfram.com/language/ref/Limit.html`.

For testing purposes, we want to display our limit equation as follows.

$$\lim_{x \to \infty} \frac{6x+1}{2x+5}$$

We can implement this equation using Mathematica as follows.

```
HoldForm[Limit[(6 x + 1)/(2 x + 5), x -> Infinity]]
```

Figure 4-23 shows the program output from this script.

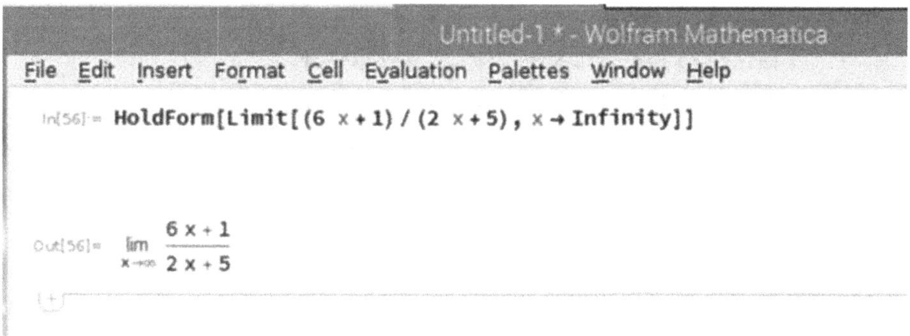

Figure 4-23. *Displaying limits*

Let's practice some more with this statement. See the following limit problems. We want to calculate these limit equations.

$$\lim_{x\to\infty}\frac{6x+1}{2x+5}$$

$$\lim_{x\to\infty}\frac{x^2}{1-x^2}$$

$$\lim_{x\to 0}\frac{\sqrt{x+25}-5}{x}$$

$$\lim_{x\to 2}\frac{x^2-7x+10}{x-2}$$

You can implement these equations in Mathematica as follows.

```
(* compute limit *)
Limit[(6 x + 1)/(2 x + 5), x -> Infinity]
Limit[x^2/(1 - x^2), x -> Infinity]
Limit[(Sqrt[x + 25] - 5)/x, x -> 0]
Limit[(x^2 - 7 x + 10)/(x - 2), x -> 2]
```

The program output of these scripts can be found in Figure 4-24.

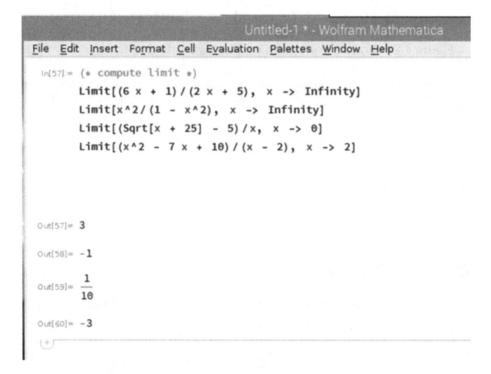

Figure 4-24. *Calculating more math limits*

4.5.1.3 Differentiation

In this section, we use differentiation. We can use the D[] syntax to implement differentiation. Read more about it at https://reference.wolfram.com/language/ref/D.html.

For testing purposes, consider the following problem.

$$f(x) = x^2$$

$$f'(x) = \frac{df}{dx} = ...??$$

The following is the implementation of this problem in Mathematica.

```
D[x^2, x]
```

Run this script. You can see the program output in Figure 4-25.

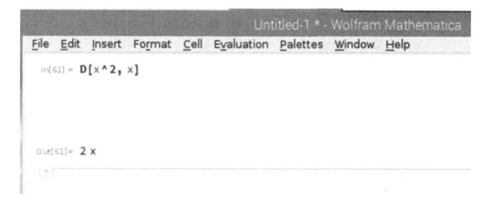

Figure 4-25. *Calculating differentiation*

Let's try some more examples. Consider the following differentiation problems.

$$f(x) = \frac{x^3}{4} + \frac{1}{x^2}$$

$$f(x) = \frac{1}{1 + \frac{1}{x}}$$

$$f(x) = x^2 e^x \cos 2x$$

$$f(x) = \log x e^x$$

A simple solution in Mathematica follows.

```
(* compute *)
D[(x^3/4) + (1/x^2), x]
D[1/(1 + 1/x), x]
D[x^2 e^x Cos[2 x], x]
D[Log[x e^x], x]
```

The program output is shown in Figure 4-26.

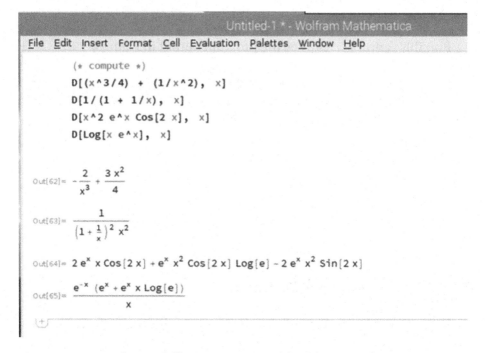

Figure 4-26. *Solving differentiation problems*

4.5.1.4 Integration

In this section, we perform two integration models—indefinite integrals and definite integrals. We explore both of these models.

4.5.1.4.1 Indefinite Integrals

First, we explore the indefinite integral. You can implement indefinite integrals using the Integrate[] statement. For more information about this statement, visit https://reference.wolfram.com/language/ref/Integrate.html.

For instance, consider the following math problems.

$$f(x)=2x$$
$$\int f(x)dx = \int 2x\,dx = \ldots??$$

You can implement this in Mathematica, using `Integrate[]` as follows.

```
Integrate[2 x, x]
```

The program output from Mathematica can be seen in Figure 4-27.

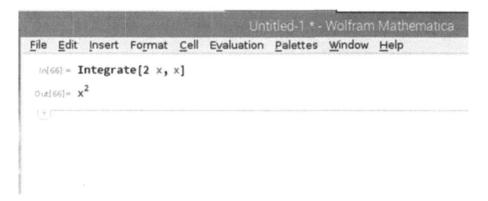

Figure 4-27. *Calculating a math integral*

Let's try some more examples. The following are more indefinite integral problems.

$$\int \frac{1}{4+3x}dx$$
$$\int \sin x \cos x\, dx$$
$$\int (\sin 3x)^2 + (\cos 3x)^2\, dx$$
$$\int (4x\ 2)^6\, dx$$

You can solve those problems in Mathematica. You can write these scripts:

```
Integrate[1/(4 + 3 x), x]
Integrate[Sin[x] Cos[x], x]
Integrate[Sin[3 x]^2 + Cos[3 x]^2, x]
Integrate[(4 x - 2)^6, x]
```

You can see the solution in Figure 4-28.

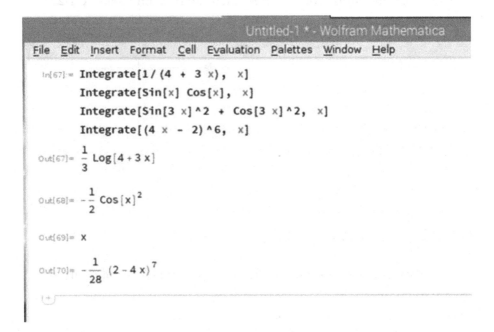

Figure 4-28. *Solving indefinite integral problems*

4.5.1.4.2 Definite Integrals

To implement a definite integral, you set the starting and ending values of the Integrate[] statement. Consider the following definite integral problems, for example.

$$\int\limits_{0}^{5} x^2\, dx$$

$$\int\limits_{0}^{1} x e^{x^2}\, dx$$

$$\int\limits_{0}^{\frac{\pi}{2}} \cos x \left(\sin x\right)^5 dx$$

$$\int\limits_{0}^{\frac{\pi}{2}} x \cos x\, dx$$

$$\int\limits_{0}^{2} \frac{1}{2x+5}\, dx$$

You can solve those problems in Mathematica as follows.

```
(* definite integral *)
Integrate[x ^2, {x, 0, 5}]
Integrate[x e^(x^2), {x, 0, 1}]
Integrate[Cos[x] Sin[x]^5, {x, 0, Pi/2}]
Integrate[x Cos[x], {x, 0, Pi/2}]
Integrate[1/(2 x + 5), {x, 0, 2}]
```

The program output is shown in Figure 4-29.

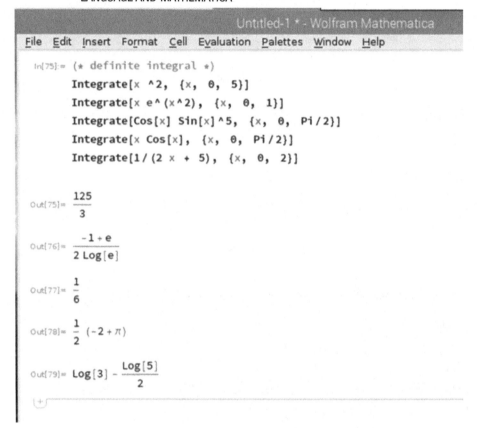

Figure 4-29. *Solving definite integral problems*

4.5.1.5 Summing

In mathematics, there are many math problems related to summation. You can use Sum[ ] to calculate sums. For further information about Sum[ ], you can visit https://reference.wolfram.com/language/ref/Sum.html.

For instance, we have a formula as follows.

$$\sum_{i=0}^{10} 2i = \ldots.??$$

You can calculate that problem using Mathematica. Write scripts in Mathematica as follows.

```
Sum[2 i, {i, 10}]
```

You can see the program output in Figure 4-30.

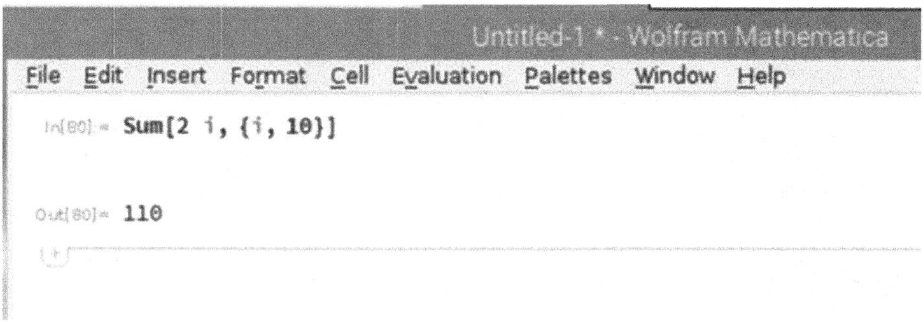

Figure 4-30. *Calculating summation in Mathematica*

Let's look at some more examples. The following are summation problems.

$$\sum_{i=5}^{10} \frac{2i-3}{5i}$$

$$\sum_{i=0}^{n} 4i$$

You can solve these problems in Mathematica. You can write these scripts.

```
Sum[(2 i - 3)/5 i, {i, 5, 10}]
Sum[4 i, {i, n}]
```

Run these scripts in Mathematica. You should get the output shown in Figure 4-31.

```
In[81]:= Sum[(2 i - 3)/5 i, {i, 5, 10}]
         Sum[4 i, {i, n}]


Out[81]= 115

Out[82]= 2 n (1 + n)
```

Figure 4-31. Solving summation problems in Mathematica

4.5.2 Matrix

In Mathematica, you can display a matrix using MatrixForm[].

For instance, say you want to display this matrix.

$$\begin{pmatrix} a \\ b \\ c \end{pmatrix}$$

$$\begin{pmatrix} 1 & 2 & 3 \\ 4 & 5 & 6 \\ 7 & 8 & 9 \end{pmatrix}$$

In Mathematica, you can formulate that matrix with the following scripts.

```
(* matrix *)
MatrixForm[{a, b, c}]
MatrixForm[{{1, 2, 3}, {4, 5, 6}, {7, 8, 9}}]
```

Run the script to see the matrix forms. The program output is shown in Figure 4-32.

132

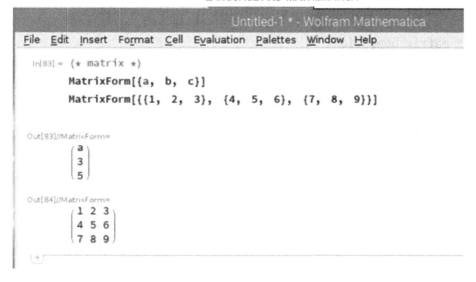

Figure 4-32. *Displaying a matrix in Mathematica*

You also can display a matrix using // MatrixForm. Write this script.

```
k = {{a, b, c}, {d, e, f}};
k // MatrixForm
```

Now we do matrix operations such as addition, subtraction, and multiplication. Consider the following cases.

$$\begin{pmatrix} 5 \\ 6 \end{pmatrix} + \begin{pmatrix} 2 & 3 \\ 4 & 2 \end{pmatrix} = \begin{pmatrix} 7 & 8 \\ 10 & 8 \end{pmatrix}$$

$$-\begin{pmatrix} 5 \\ 6 \end{pmatrix} + \begin{pmatrix} 2 & 3 \\ 4 & 2 \end{pmatrix} = \begin{pmatrix} -3 & -2 \\ -2 & -4 \end{pmatrix}$$

$$\begin{pmatrix} 2 & 3 \\ 4 & 2 \end{pmatrix} \cdot \begin{pmatrix} 5 \\ 6 \end{pmatrix} = \begin{pmatrix} 28 \\ 32 \end{pmatrix}$$

You can implement them in Mathematica scripts as follows.

```
(* matrix operations *)
Clear[m, n];
m = {{2, 3}, {4, 2}};
n = {5, 6};
(n // MatrixForm) + (m // MatrixForm) == (m + n // MatrixForm)
(m // MatrixForm) - (n // MatrixForm) == (m - n // MatrixForm)
(m // MatrixForm) . (n // MatrixForm) == (m . n // MatrixForm)
```

The program output is shown in Figure 4-33.

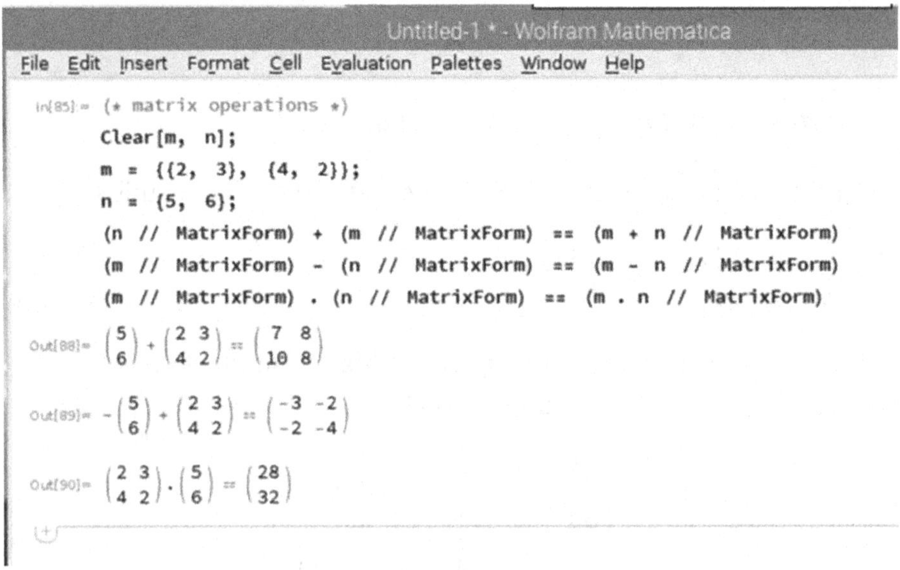

Figure 4-33. *Solving matrix operations*

If you want to transpose a matrix, you can use Transpose[ ].
For instance, consider this matrix as an example.

$$\begin{pmatrix} 2 & 3 & 4 \\ 5 & 6 & 7 \end{pmatrix}$$

You can transpose this matrix with the following scripts.

```
(* Transpose *)
L = {{2, 3, 4}, {5, 6, 7}};
L // MatrixForm
Transpose[L] // MatrixForm
```

Run these scripts and you should get program output shown in
Figure 4-34.

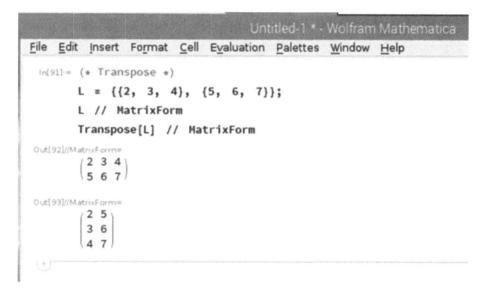

Figure 4-34. *Transposing a matrix*

You can find determinants, inverses, and matrix ranks from a matrix as
well. For instance, consider this matrix.

$$\begin{pmatrix} 2 & 4 \\ 7 & 8 \end{pmatrix}$$

To calculate a determinant, inverse, and rank using Mathematica, you would use the following scripts:

```
(* Determinant *)
A = {{2, 4}, {7, 8}};
A // MatrixForm
Det[A]
Inverse[A] // MatrixForm
MatrixRank[A]
```

The program output from these scripts can be seen in Figure 4-35.

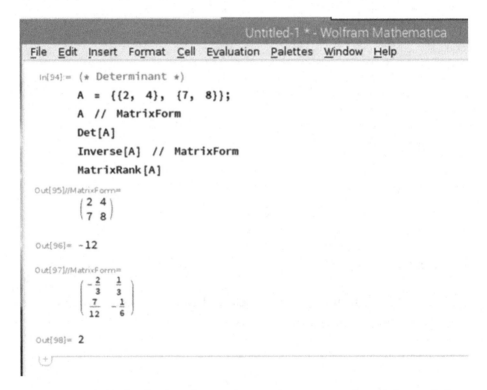

Figure 4-35. *Calculating determinant, inverse, and matrix rank from a matrix*

4.5.3 Quadratic Equations

We find values of unknown parameters in quadratic equations using
Solve[]. For more information about the Solve[] statement, visit
https://reference.wolfram.com/language/ref/Solve.html.

For instance, we have the quadratic equation shown here.

$$x^2 - 3x \ 4 = 0$$

Now we can find the x values using Solve[].

```
(* Quadratic Equations *)
Solve[x^2 - 3 x - 4 == 0, x]
```

Run the program and you will see that the x values are -1 and 4.
The program output is shown in Figure 4-36.

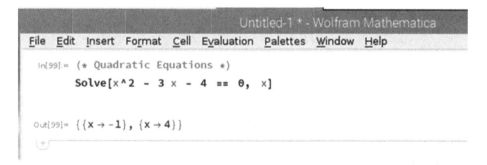

Figure 4-36. *Solving quadratic equations*

Let's look at some other examples. The following are quadratic
equation problems. Find the x values.

$$x^2 - 4 = 0$$
$$6x^2 + 11x - 35 = 0$$
$$x^2 - 7x = 0$$

Those problems can be solved in Mathematica. You can write these scripts to solve for x.

```
Solve[x^2 - 4 == 0, x]
Solve[6 x^2 + 11 x - 35 == 0, x]
Solve[x^2 - 7 x == 0, x]
```

The program output from Mathematica can be seen in Figure 4-37.

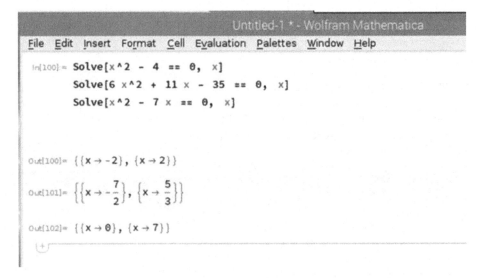

Figure 4-37. *Quadratic equation solutions in Mathematica*

4.5.4 Linear Equations

In linear equations, we solve to find values from a set of parameters. We can use the Solve[] statement in Mathematica to do this. For more information about this statement, visit https://reference.wolfram.com/language/ref/Solve.html.

For instance, we have three equations:

$$x + y + z = 0$$
$$x + 2y + 3z = 1$$
$$x - y + z = 2$$

We can find the x, y, and z values in Mathematica.

```
Solve[{x + y + z, x + 2 y + 3 z, x - y + z} == {0, 1, 2}]
```

Another problem you can solve is as follows.

$$3x - y = 0$$
$$y + 2z = 1$$
$$x + y + z = 3$$

The solutions from these problems in Mathematica are as follows.

```
Solve[{3 x - y, y + 2 z, x + y + z} == {0, 1, 3}]
```

Run all these scripts. You'll see the program output in Figure 4-38.

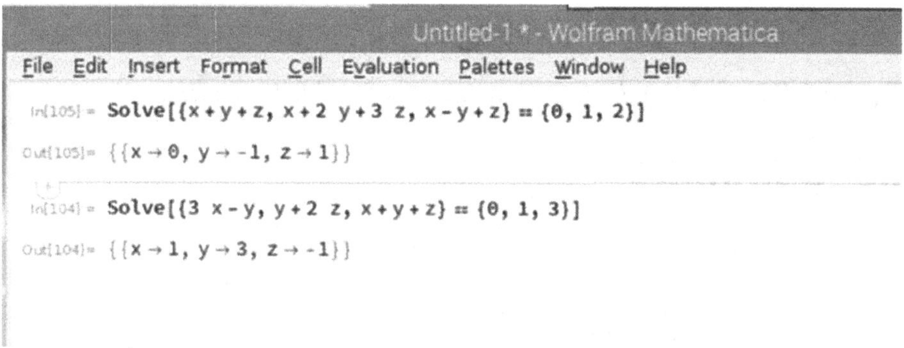

Figure 4-38. *Solving linear equations using Mathematica*

You can see the x, y, and z values.

Now we have another problem. The w parameter shown here is a constant value.

$$2x + 3y - 7z + w = 8$$
$$4x - 2y + z + 2w = 4$$
$$5x + y - 4z + 3w = 6$$

The solutions are written in Mathematica, as shown in the following script.

```
Solve[{2 x + 3 y - 7 z + w, 4 x - 2 y + z + 2 w, 5 x + y - 4 z + 3 w} == {8, 4, 6}]
```

The program output can be seen in Figure 4-39.

Figure 4-39. *Solving linear equations using Mathematica*

4.6 Summary

In this chapter, you learned about the Wolfram and Mathematica programs in Raspbian OS that run on Raspberry Pi boards. You also played math games such as computational mathematics to see how to work with Mathematica.

In the next chapter, we focus on visual programming using Scratch on the Raspbian OS and Raspberry Pi boards.

CHAPTER 5

Visual Programming with Scratch

Scratch is a visual programming application that you can use to write programs visually. In this chapter, we explore the Scratch application by creating blocks to build programs visually.

The following is a list of topics covered in this chapter:

- Learn about visual programming

- Set up Scratch

- Develop a hello program

- Work with Sprites

- Work with backgrounds

- Work with motion

- Work with controls

© Agus Kurniawan 2019
A. Kurniawan, *Raspbian OS Programming with the Raspberry Pi,*
https://doi.org/10.1007/978-1-4842-4212-4_5

5.1 Introducing Visual Programming and Scratch

Visual programming is a programming method that you can use to develop programs without writing codes/scripts directly. You can click and drag components or modules into the board and the tool will generate codes from your visual models.

In this chapter, we explore visual programming with Scratch. Scratch is a free desktop and online multimedia authoring tool that can be used by students, scholars, teachers, and parents to easily create games. It provides a stepping-stone to the more advanced world of computer programming. It can even be used for a range of educational and entertainment purposes, from math and science projects, including simulations and visualizations of experiments, recording lectures with animated presentations, to social sciences animated stories, and interactive art and music. See Figure 5-1.

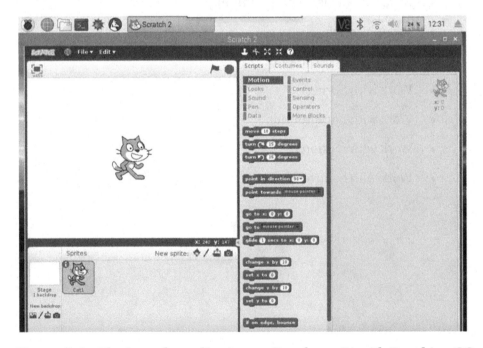

Figure 5-1. *The Scratch application on Raspberry Pi with Raspbian OS*

5.2 Setting Up Scratch

By default, the Scratch application has been installed in the Raspbian desktop on the Raspberry Pi board. You can access the Scratch and Scratch 2 applications from the Programming menu, which is on the main menu (see Figure 5-2).

In this chapter, we only explore the Scratch 2 application. We learn how to build and run programs.

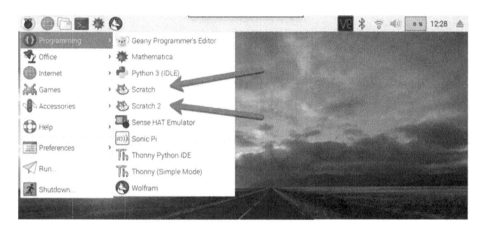

Figure 5-2. *The Scratch application on the main menu*

5.3 Developing a Hello Program

In this section, you see how to build a Scratch program for a hello world application. Follow the steps in the next sections.

5.3.1 Creating a Project

First, open the Scratch application and create a new program by choosing File ➤ New, as shown in Figure 5-3.

143

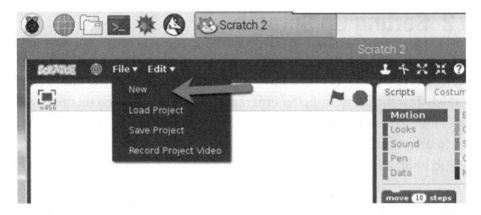

Figure 5-3. *Creating a new project*

You'll get a blank script, as shown in Figure 5-4.

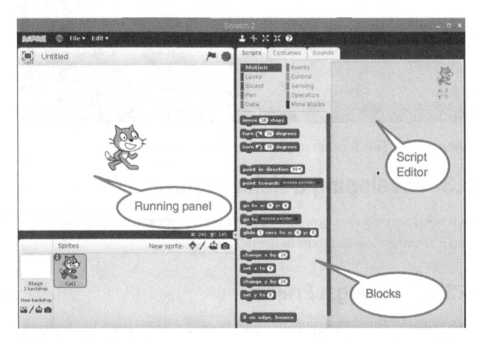

Figure 5-4. *The Scratch Editor*

Figure 5-4 shows the Scratch Editor. You build Scratch programs using the Script Editor panel. All the blocks that are used to develop Scratch programs can be taken from the Blocks panel. Each block is collected into a group.

- Motion

- Looks

- Sound

- Pen

- Data

- Events

- Control

- Sensing

- Operators

You can simply click and drag from the Blocks panel to the Script Editor. Last, you can see a running panel that shows how your program runs.

5.3.2 Building a Scratch Program

For demo purposes, this example shows the "Hello Raspberry Pi" text on the sprite when it's clicked. Click Events from the palates area (on the Scripts tab). You will see a list of Scratch blocks for the Events blocks, as shown in Figure 5-5.

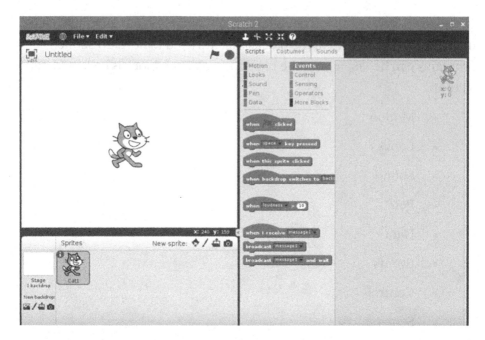

Figure 5-5. *Listing the blocks on Events*

Click the When "Green Flag" Clicked block. Click and hold it to move it to the Script Editor. You can see the result in Figure 5-6.

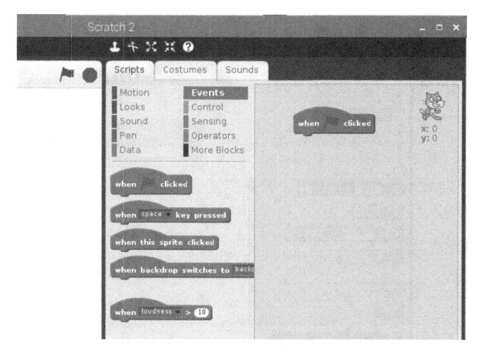

Figure 5-6. *Adding a block to the Script Editor*

Now click Looks from the Scripts tab. You will see the Say "Hello!" block. Click and hold it. Then, move it into the editor. You can see the result in Figure 5-7.

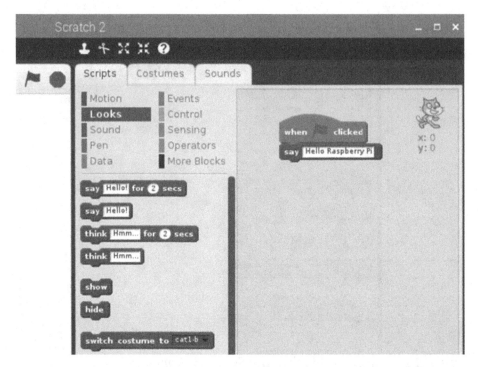

Figure 5-7. *Adding the Say "Hello" block*

Change the text from "Hello" to "Hello Raspberry Pi". You have officially created your first Scratch program. Now you are ready to run it.

5.3.3 Running the Program

To run a Scratch program, you can click the Green Flag icon on the top-right of the running panel. After it's clicked, you should see the message "Hello Raspberry Pi" spoken by the Sprite cat. You can see these results in Figure 5-8.

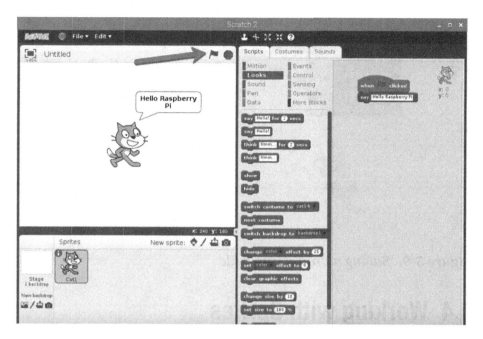

Figure 5-8. *An example of running a Scratch program*

5.3.4 Saving a Program Into a File

If you want to save a Scratch program, you can do so by choosing File ➤ Save Project, as shown in Figure 5-9. You will get a dialog box to store the Scratch program file. Fill in the filename of your project. When you're done, click the OK button.

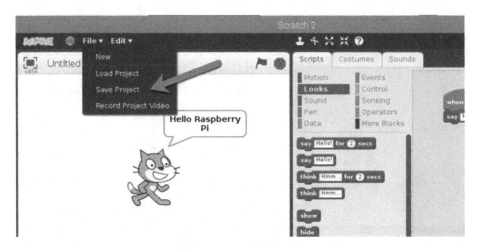

Figure 5-9. *Saving a project into a file*

5.4 Working with Sprites

If you see a character image on the running panel, it is a sprite. You can change the sprites in your program. To change your sprite, click the sprite icon in Figure 5-10.

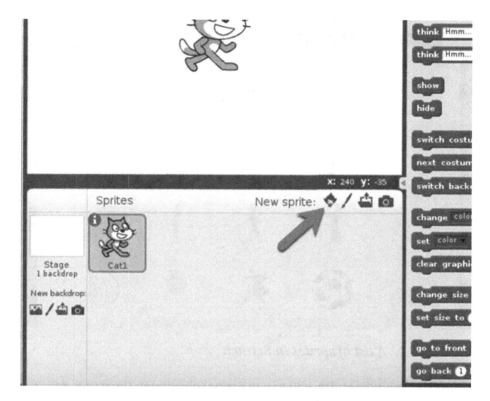

Figure 5-10. *Adding a new sprite*

After you click this icon, you'll see a list of sprites, as shown in Figure 5-11. You can select one of your favorite Sprites.

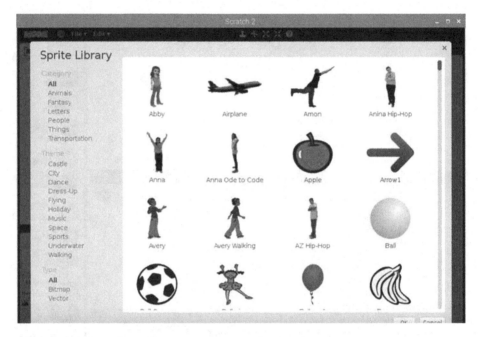

Figure 5-11. *A list of sprites in Scratch*

After selecting a sprite, you can see your selection in the panel, as shown in Figure 5-12.

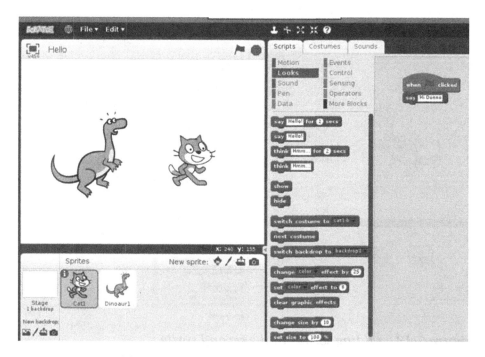

Figure 5-12. *Adding additional sprites to the panel*

When you click a sprite on the bottom-left panel, you should see the Script Editor. This means each sprite has own Scratch program. For demo purposes, add the same scripts as the previous sprite script. You can see my script code for the second sprite in Figure 5-13.

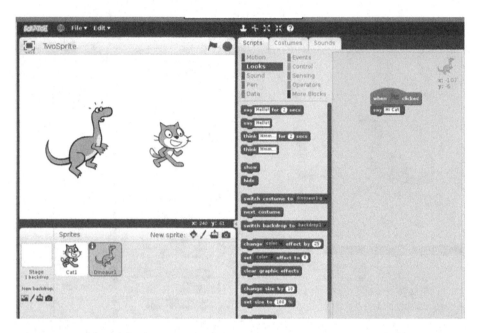

Figure 5-13. *Adding scripts to the second sprite*

Now click the Green Flag icon to run this demo. You can see my demo in Figure 5-14.

Figure 5-14. *Running a Scratch program with two sprites*

5.5 Working with the Background

You also can change the Scratch program background. First, you need to add a background file by clicking the image icon. See the arrow in Figure 5-15.

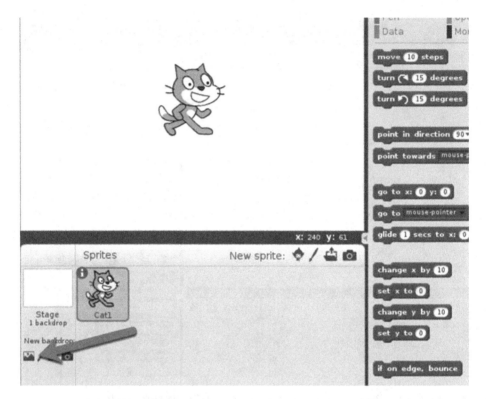

Figure 5-15. *Clicking the image icon*

After it's been clicked, you should get a dialog that displays a list of backgrounds. You can see this list in Figure 5-16.

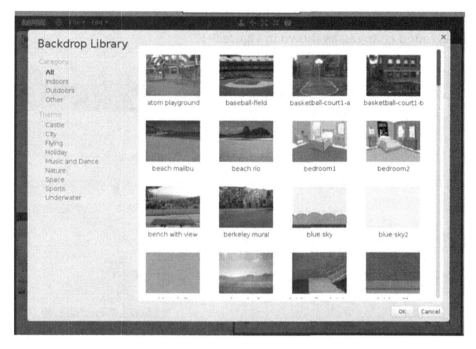

Figure 5-16. *A list of backgrounds for your Scratch programs*

After you select a background, you should see that the current panel background changes, as shown in Figure 5-17.

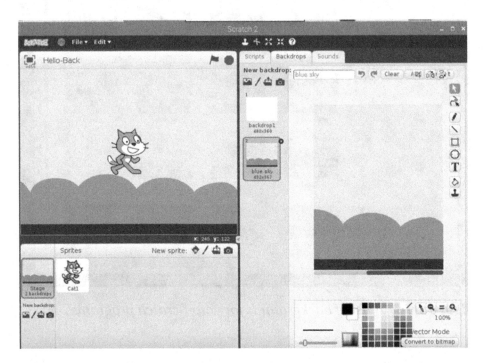

Figure 5-17. *A Scratch program with a custom background*

If you use the first demo Scratch program and try to run it, you should see the program output shown in Figure 5-18.

Figure 5-18. *A hello Scratch program with a custom*
background

5.6 Working with Motion

In this section, you learn to move your sprites using the Motion palette.
You can see the Motion palette in Figure 5-19.

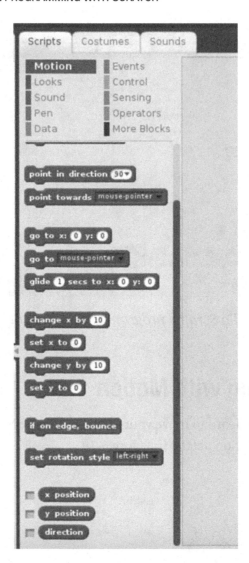

Figure 5-19. *A list of blocks in the Motion palette*

5.6.1 Coordinate System and Direction

To move a sprite in a stage, you first need to understand how coordinate systems work on the stage. For instance, you can see a sprite in a stage, shown in Figure 5-20.

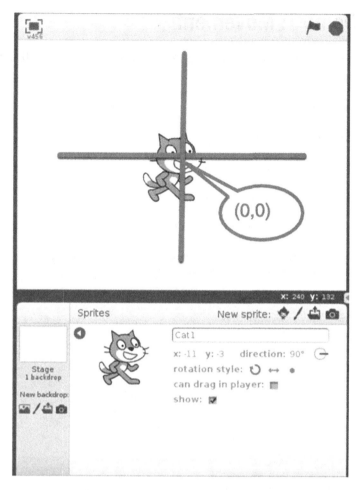

Figure 5-20. *The coordinate system on Scratch*

Point (0,0) is located on the middle of the stage. You can move this sprite using your mouse by clicking and holding the sprite. You can also get information about the sprite location, for instance, a sprite is located at x=0, y=0.

You can change the sprite direction by clicking and holding the sprite. Then move it using the mouse. Then, you can see the sprite direction output on the stage.

5.6.2 Demo 1: Movement

This demo shows you how to move a sprite on the stage. The following is our scenario:

- A sprite starts on x=0, y=0

- Move it 10 steps

- Move it another 10 steps

- Turn direction about 45 degrees

The program implementation can be seen in Figure 5-21.

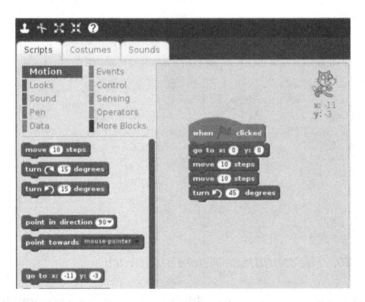

Figure 5-21. *Implementing a movement program*

Save this program into a project file. To run it, you can simply click the Green Flag icon. You can see an example of the project output in Figure 5-22.

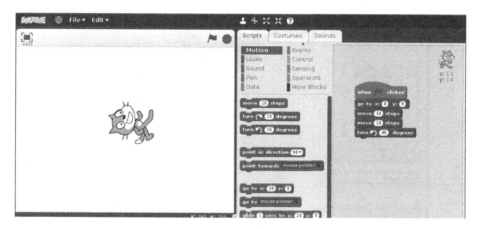

Figure 5-22. *Running the Scratch application*

5.6.3 Demo 2: Direction

The second demo builds a program for changing the sprite's direction. Our scenario is defined as follows:

- Change the sprite's direction 90 degrees

- Move the sprite from x=0, y=0

- Glide the sprite to x=300, y=0

- Add a conditional whereby, if the sprite is on an edge position, it will bounce

For implementation, you can build the program shown in Figure 5-23.

163

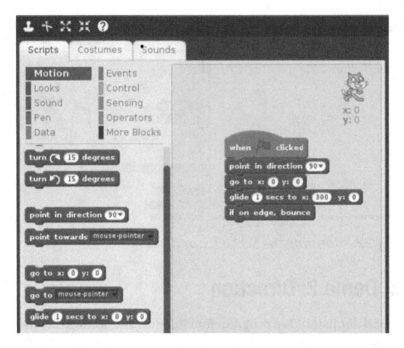

Figure 5-23. *Scratch program for demo 2*

Save this program into a project file. To run it, click the Green Flag icon.
See Figure 5-24.

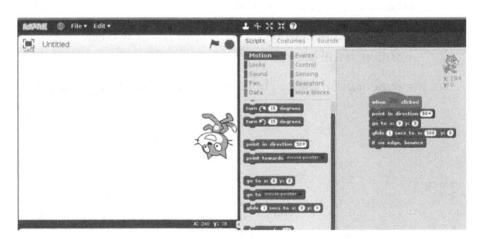

Figure 5-24. *Running a Scratch program for direction*

5.7 Working with Control Blocks

You can see many different items on the Control palette. Technically, these items consist of decision and looping actions. In this chapter, we explore how to build Scratch programs using the decision and looping actions.

5.7.1 Building a Decision

To build a decision, you can use `if..else` command, which is located on the Control palette. You can see a list of blocks on the Control palette in Figure 5-25.

For demo purposes, we build a Scratch app with the following features:

- Define two variables, numA and numB

- Set a random value for numA and numB

- Check and compare numA and numB

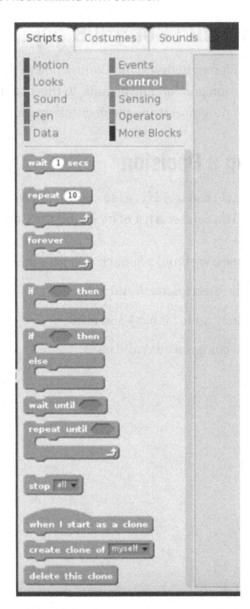

Figure 5-25. *Blocks on the Control palette*

To implement the program, you can follow these instructions.

First, drag the When "Green Flag" Clicked block to the Script Editor. Next, you need to define the variables, called numA and numB, which can be found on the Data blocks. See Figure 5-26.

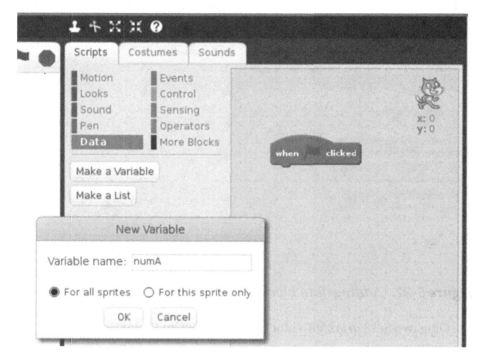

Figure 5-26. *Defining the variables*

When you're done, you can see your two variables. You can also see blocks related to your variables in Figure 5-27.

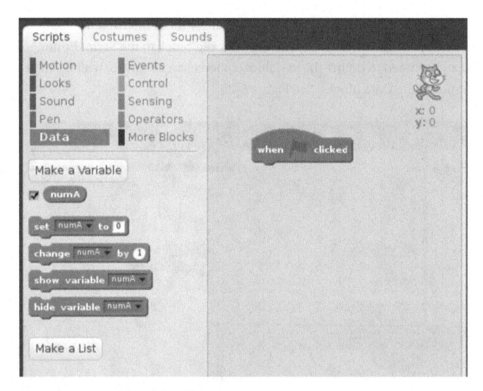

Figure 5-27. *Adding data blocks*

Drag two Set *Variable* To blocks onto the Script Editor, as shown in Figure 5-28.

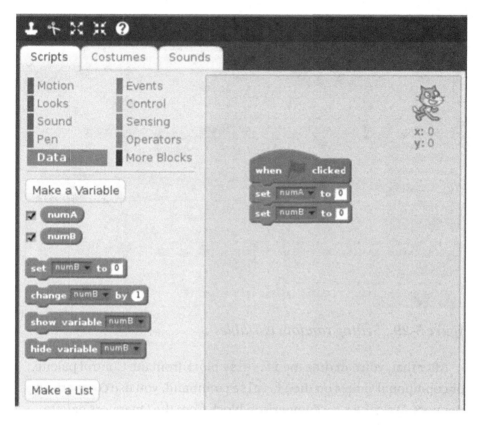

Figure 5-28. *Putting variables on the editor*

Replace the variable values, numA and numB, with the Pick Random 1 To 10 block from the Operators category. See Figure 5-29.

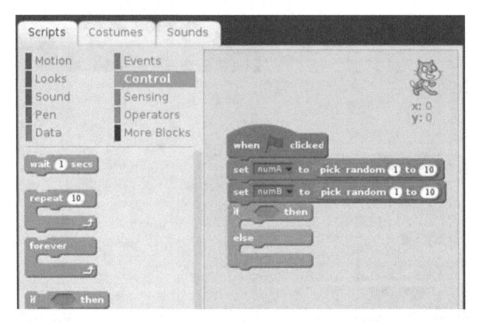

Figure 5-29. *Setting random variables*

After that, you can drag the `if..else` block from the Control palette. For conditional values on the `if..else` command, you use comparison operators. Drag the x < y comparison block from the Operators palette. Assign if-conditional to the numA and numB variables. The resulting form can be seen in Figure 5-30.

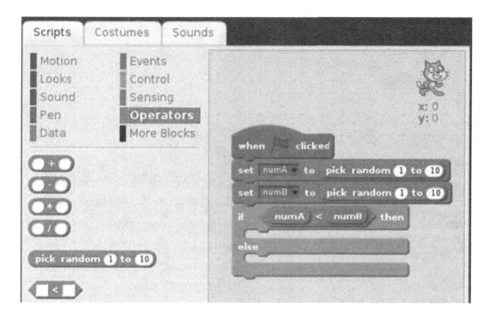

Figure 5-30. *Adding an if-else block*

Now add Say "B is bigger" and "A is bigger" to the responses for the if..else command. As an example, you can see my script form in Figure 5-31.

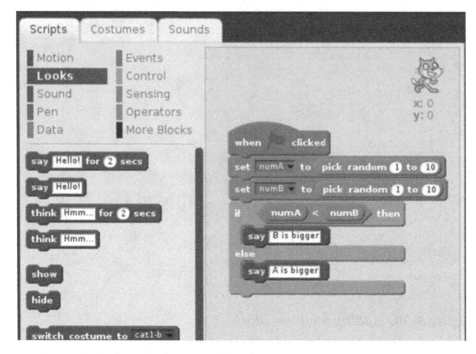

Figure 5-31. *Adding an if-else block*

Save this program into a project file. Run this program by clicking the Green Flag icon. Figure 5-32 shows the result.

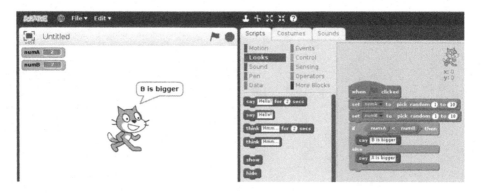

Figure 5-32. *Running Scratch program with if-else block*

5.7.2 Looping

There are many options for building a Scratch program using looping. You can see them in Figure 5-33.

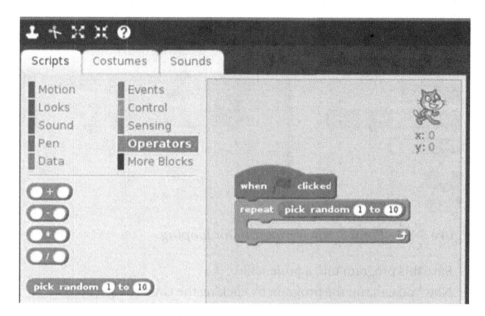

Figure 5-33. *Putting the Repeat block into the script*

For demo purposes, you'll build a program that loops a random value. First, drag the When "Green Flag" Clicked block from the Events palette. Then, drag the Repeat 10 block from the Control palette. The resulting form is shown in Figure 5-33.

Change the 10 value using the Pick Random 1 to 10 block from the Operators palette. Last, you can drag the Say Hello! for 2 Secs block inside of the Repeat Command block. You can see the resulting script in Figure 5-34.

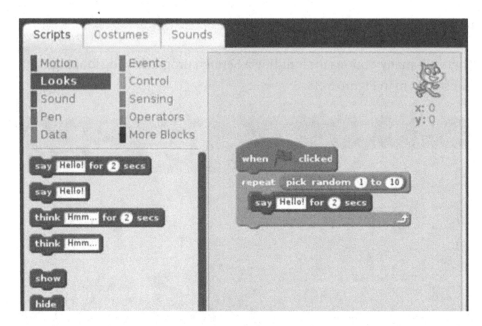

Figure 5-34. *Final Scratch program for looping*

Save this program into a project file.

Now you can run the program by clicking the Green Flag icon. The program will display Hello! x times (x is a random value from 1 to 10). You can see my running program in Figure 5-35.

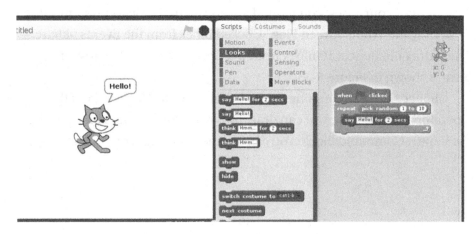

Figure 5-35. *Running the looping program in Scratch*

What's next?

It's a good idea to practice more with the various script blocks in Scratch. You also can see project examples that people have uploaded onto the Scratch website at `https://scratch.mit.edu`.

5.8 Summary

In this chapter, you learned how to work with the Scratch application to develop programs visually. The chapter reviewed several blocks—such as sprites, backgrounds, motions, and control blocks—and you were able to run many examples for practice. Visit the official website, `https://scratch.mit.edu`, to get inspired and to develop your own Scratch programs.

Index

© Agus Kurniawan 2019
A. Kurniawan, *Raspbian OS Programming with the Raspberry Pi*,
https://doi.org/10.1007/978-1-4842-4212-4

Printed in the United States
By Bookmasters